A highly unlikely
bicycle tourist

A highly unlikely bicycle tourist

STEPHEN PEEL

A highly unlikely bicycle tourist
Copyright © 2020 Stephen Peel

All rights reserved. No part of this book may be reproduced in any form or by any electronic or mechanical means, including information storage and retrieval systems, without written permission from the author, except in the case of a reviewer, who may quote brief passages embodied in critical articles or a review.

Cover photograph and internal photographs – Stephen Peel

Author – Stephen Peel

ISBN: 978-1-8380644-0-2 (colour paperback)
ISBN: 978-1-8380644-1-9 (black and white paperback)
ISBN: 978-1-8380644-2-6 (colour hardback)
ISBN: 978-1-8380644-3-3 (ebook)

Many an incredible story may have been told about young courageous men and women cycling the globe in search of adventure, covering vast distances at speed each day with not a care in the world, sleeping wherever they could pitch a tent or find someone willing to give them a free meal and bed for the night, who intentionally looked bedraggled to resemble famous adventurers of old, with men sporting wild hair and beards that could clear dusty streets as they cycled through.

Well, this incredible story is a little different. It is an astonishing story about a 350-pound middle-aged, disabled, working-class husband and father. I was never a regular cyclist, and I knew nothing about bicycle maintenance and repair. And yet, without a single day of bicycle touring practice, I loaded up my shiny new bike with everything I thought I'd need and cycled out of Cheshire to see the world. Solo, self-financed, with no support network and without any fixed route plan other than, "I'm going that way."

What could go wrong? I wondered.

To those who made me smile, laugh,
took an interest in what I was doing,
helped when I needed help,
THANK YOU

Contents

CHAPTER 1

Being soaked to the bone was no fun at all

Built like a brick shithouse as a result of decades of heavy manual labour in the building industry and weight training, and a bacon butty or two, cycling had never been my hobby.

In 2016, my doctor suggested that an occasional short bicycle ride would relieve some pain in my lower back. So I took his advice and bought a cheap, second-hand bike. I was 53 years old at the time and hadn't owned a bicycle for decades. I lived near the coast in Tanlan, North Wales, where I started taking occasional short rides along a coastal promenade and pathways, avoiding roads as best I could.

I enjoyed cycling for a few miles to grab a coffee at a café on the prom and chat with a few people I met along the way from time to time. Every so often, I'd talk with young bicycle tourists who were following the coastline, and I loved to hear all about their adventures as it seemed a great way to travel.

I started reading bicycle touring stories written mostly by middle-class, university-educated young people with support networks at home, few responsibilities, and even sponsorship in some cases.

Although I admired those young people for their achievements and bicycle touring contributions, I wanted to hear from parents and spouses and the middle-aged working-class like me. After a little digging on some social media platforms, I found that people of all ages and backgrounds were on incredible adventures all over the world.

There were people on unicycles, tricycles, bikes with trailers, and all manner of unusual pedal-powered contraptions. Some people were in their twilight years, and a few had disabilities. Others were travelling for just a few days or weeks, but some for much longer. Interestingly, a few were not only seeking adventure, but were hoping to find the reason for their entire being.

I hadn't had my hybrid bicycle for long when my wife, Sue, and I moved to England. I was still 53 years old and couldn't get the idea of riding a bike from country to country out of my head. I was inspired by Mark Beaumont's video of his record-breaking cycle around the world. Mark told me in an email that, "There is no better pace to see the world," and from what I'd read, I could believe it. So I decided to take my doctor's "occasional short ride" suggestion to the next illogical level. I was between jobs and had saved enough money not to have to rely on the goodwill or charity of others, but I felt I wouldn't knock the goodwill or charity back if offered.

I told my wife and daughters, Chelsea and Chloe, about my vague plan, which was to ride out of Cheshire and the UK, and just keep going. My daughters thought it would have been a good idea to take a shorter ride first, such as the length of Great Britain from Land's End to John O'Groats. But I wanted to see how far and for how long I could ride without any bicycle touring or bicycle maintenance experience. I thought it would add to the adventure, and I was excited at the thought of learning as I went. A few people I had spoken with said I wouldn't get very far without a good deal of practice and some repair and maintenance skills. But their can't-do attitude made me more determined to go ahead with my plan. I planned to keep going until something beyond my control stopped me, or I felt I had done what I wanted to do. I might have ruled out practicing, but I still had to prepare in other ways. I imagined a bicycle tour of just a few weeks requiring few financial risks and minimal planning.

In contrast, a trip of what could be many months or years would be a completely different beast. I would have to write a will and get a new passport with plenty of extra pages, just in case. I'd need treatments against viruses and other illnesses, such as rabies, yellow fever and malaria. I had no idea where I might end up, so I thought it would be a good idea to be covered. I would also have to work out what clothing I might need, and I had no doubt the list of equipment would be lengthy.

I started looking at bikes I thought would do the job, and it was fun but challenging. I needed the equivalent of a Shire horse, not a racehorse. I needed a bike that could carry my bulk and about 100 pounds of gear. It would have to be super strong to take all that weight over not just roads, but tracks and trails too, and it would also have to be easy to maintain and reliable. I couldn't find a single bike that had a weight limit compatible with me. After a lot of reading about the pros and cons of different bicycles and parts, I chose the KOGA WorldTraveller bicycle. But at more than £4,000 with the panniers and spares, it wasn't cheap.

After ordering the bike from Cyclesense in Tadcaster, North Yorkshire, I bought all the gear I thought I'd need and then some. The gear I was taking weighed 143 pounds, and the total weight, including me, was just shy of 500 pounds.

The night before the first day of my tour, my mum was feeling a bit upset and worried. Sue and I were living in Liverpool, less than 20 miles from Mum, so I decided to spend the evening with her and leave from there the following morning. Chelsea and Chloe lived nearby, so I was also able to see them that evening too.

I had already said goodbye to Sue, which I thought was a good idea instead of letting her realise I was gone when the lawns had grown three feet deep. I promised her I'd phone each day if I could, and hopefully have her fly out to spend a little time with me at some point, somewhere. Sue wasn't happy about my adventure, and she was worried something terrible might happen. She planned to keep herself busy, and I made sure she had a new push lawnmower, lots of new gardening tools, and a big toolkit and drill. *What more could she need?* I thought.

After a restless sleep on Mum's settee, I carried out the last checks on the bike to make sure I had everything and that it was all secure. I had no idea how the bike was going to feel or handle with the bags fully loaded, and I couldn't be sure all the weight wouldn't buckle the wheels if I hit a pothole in the road. The bike with all the gear on looked ready for anything. It was the 1st of August 2017, when I said goodbye to my teary mum as she stood in her doorway out of the rain in the dull early morning light.

Just one mile into my ride I stopped on a footbridge, from where I could see the streets where my daughters lived, and I imagined them sound asleep. It upset me, and tears welled up in my eyes. I felt my chest tighten as I said, "Goodbye, I love you," under my breath before I cycled on, with the rain hiding my tears as they rolled off my face. I had no idea when I would see my wife and children again.

Less than five miles into my journey, I bumped into an old friend, Fran. I hadn't seen him for decades, and he was crossing the same bridge but going the other way on his bicycle to work. It was great to see him and chat for a few minutes. A little farther on, I passed a roadside café and the thought of a full English breakfast and getting out of the rain for a few minutes seemed like a good plan, so I turned around and filled up. That first day, I cycled 24 miles in the rain to Yatehouse Farm Camping in Middlewich. Once there, I eagerly set about pitching the tent and inflating the air mattress and pillow.

It felt great to put everything together for the first time. I had previously set the tent up in the garden to make sure it was complete and undamaged, but I hadn't slept in a tent for more than 15 years so I was like a big kid. I also bought a gear-shed attachment, which was a small extra room that clipped onto the frame of the main tent. It added a lot of extra space to keep wet clothing and the bike out of sight when wild camping. It also meant I'd have more room in the main tent area away from anything soaking wet. I had no use for the gear-shed on the campsite; the bike was given a place in a greenhouse, and locked to a table.

The campsite owner looked at the sign hanging off the rear of my Ortlieb rack-pack. It had details of JUMP, the charity I had chosen to support on my ride. It also displayed my website address and social media channels. He asked if I was going to cycle completely around the world. I told him I hadn't ruled it out. He went on to ask how far I'd cycled. I told him it was my first day, and he burst out laughing, then I burst out laughing with him because I must have looked like I'd been cycling for months. He handed me a bag of fruit and said I could stay at the campsite free of charge, which was kind.

While preparing for my adventure, I felt that, because I was doing something so big, it would be nice to support my local charity at the same time. JUMP supports children with life-limiting illnesses. It arranges days out for the children and their families. Videos and books are created, so the families have something extra to remember their children by if or when the children sadly pass away.

The ground was soaking wet, so I thought it would be a great idea to pitch the tent under a tree for shelter. During the night, rainwater would build on the leaves before being released and shaking the branches. I drifted off quickly, despite the heavy rain. I soon awoke to what I could only describe as a feeling of someone pushing a long knife straight through my right thigh, and I yelped in excruciating pain. It jolted me so severely that I hurt my back in the process of sitting up too quickly in the restricted space of my sleeping bag. I was then feeling pain in my back, and cramp in my left leg which just seemed to appear for good measure. Neither of those extra pains came close to the pain in my right thigh.

Once the thigh pain eased, I lay on my back for a few minutes but it started again, and I struggled to hold my voice from waking other campers. I raised and squeezed my knee until the pain went away, but the pain came back. I thought I'd torn a muscle from doing far too much on my first day and had ended my adventure while still in Cheshire. I was devastated. I lay there feeling more than a little sorry for myself and soon fell asleep. I awoke the next morning in a large puddle of rainwater because my tent was in a dip but, on the plus side, the thigh pain had pretty much gone, so I decided to continue. My first day had turned out far harder than I had thought possible, and all I could think about was my daughters suggesting I should have had some practice.

It was still raining as I set out, and the wind was coming hard at me. I managed 28 miles, which was a massive achievement for me as I hadn't ridden that kind of distance since my teens. I was so tired. I booked into a hotel because I couldn't find a campsite within reach, and I was at least able to wash and dry some clothes and have a hot meal.

Being soaked to the bone was no fun at all, but only to be expected in England in the height of summer! My waterproof clothing didn't help much because it was the type trawler people sometimes used out at sea: thick, heavy rubber. I was too big to be able to buy cycling or sports waterproof clothing or most other types of clothing, so I had to wear whatever I could buy online. My shoulder width resulted in long sleeves being short sleeves, and I was aware that being up to 5XL might cause all kinds of problems as I progressed through my adventure. Trying to squeeze into Lycra was like trying to get 350 pounds of sausage meat into a 200-pound sausage skin, which was not a pretty sight. I wore baggy shorts over the top to save people's blushes and my own. I could picture towns like those hosting Wild West shootouts, with mothers dragging their children and pets off the streets and closing the shutters as I passed through. Maybe a little exaggeration, but I had myself laughing at the thought.

Soothing new-found muscles and getting into a big, sprung bed that second night was pure bliss. I had every faith that, at some point, my muscles would settle in, the sun would shine, and I would become less embarrassed about how I looked in tight clothing.

The following day, as I cycled along a canal towpath, I came across some young bulls stuck in the water up to their middles. The rest of the herd stood around, unable to do anything but stare. I pedalled on at a good pace for three miles in the rain until I came to a pub and approached the manager. It turned out she knew who owned the young bulls and told me everything would be fine, so I continued on my way towards a campsite I had located. The rain was relentless and I was still suffering sore muscles, though I had another feeling I hadn't expected to feel so soon: a sense of real freedom. I had everything with me I thought I'd need to see my adventure through, and no time constraints.

I'd had nothing but horrid weather since leaving home, but finally, I had a day with the wind to my back and a few breaks in the clouds. I felt good, even taking into account the bone and butt-shaking experience of cycling on the mostly narrow tracks that made up much of the canal tow-path. Later that morning, I cycled right through the middle of a beautiful wheat field on a flattened path a tractor had made. I stood the bike in the middle and snapped an image I thought would always remind me of my adventure. I also thought it would look good on a book cover although, at that time, I hadn't written anything longer than a high school essay, and I was no poet either.

It rained all night, and in the morning I had to beat everyone on the campsite to the washroom dryers. If I hadn't made it to the dryers first, I could have been waiting for hours in a queue or I might have had to hit the road with everything wet and weighty. Thankfully, I got everything dry. A lady named Sue and her son Kai had set up their tent with some friends next to mine the night before, and they made me a nice brew before I packed up and set off.

Wild camping was something I was looking forward to, though I didn't expect to be doing it so soon. I felt sure I'd have no trouble finding campsites. My problem was not being able to cover vast distances each day so, for me, campsites were few and far between. If my range had been between 50 and 100 miles a day, I would have stood a much better chance. That first night of wild camping was at the end of a very long and hard day; a typical day at that point. I struggled over my first bumps and hills, and I eventually ran out of steam.

I stood at an opening in a hedge that led to a farmer's recently cut field. I couldn't see anyone nearby, so I waited for the last cars to pass before quickly pushing the bike through the gap and setting up my tent behind the hedge, out of sight. It felt nice to get out of my sweat-soaked, heavy clothing, followed by a scrub with a packet of baby wipes, before diving into a dry sleeping bag.

I attached the gear-shed to the tent and hid the bike inside, along with everything else I didn't need in the main tent area. Weight, space, weather resistance and strength were all critical factors when choosing a tent, so I had done a lot of research before selecting the MSR Hubba Hubba NX. Being extra-large, I had decided on the two-person version.

Cooking was not on the cards at that point, because I rarely cooked a proper meal at home when on my own. I would grab snacks or make something simple instead. I could appreciate how nice it would have been for a couple of people to finish a ride, put a pan on and cook some simple food, then sit chatting for a while before crashing out for the night. Cooking a meal for one behind a hedge in a field didn't sound like fun to me. It sounded more like a chore, followed by washing the dishes and tidying everything up.

The next morning I was back on a towpath. It was often hard work when a towpath turned to a narrow, muddy trail, so I struggled a bit but managed to keep from falling in the water. I had passed a lot of cyclists since setting out. Or rather, a lot had passed me, but I also came across my first bicycle tourist, Lara. She had been cycling for days in the opposite direction to me. We had a good chat. It was great to hear about her adventure and how she'd spent days on her own. Solo long-distance cyclists always impressed me.

Before I started my adventure, I saw some photos of a bicycle tourist in Africa who had covered his frame in foam tubing. He talked about how he had to carry his bike at times, and the tubing protected his shoulders. He said it also made the bike look a bit strange and it might have put people off stealing it. I thought I'd give it a try, and I found it quite comfortable when I had to straddle the bike at a stop.

Stopping for a bite to eat and drink at The Red Lion in Hunningham was nice. I felt the setting was lovely. There was a stream running under an old stone bridge, and I just had to take a snap. The foam tubing looked sort of weird, I guess, but I liked it.

I'd been on the road for nearly a week, and it was a great feeling to make it to Banbury, between Coventry and Oxford. Later the next day, I stopped at a grocery shop owned by a Sri Lankan family that had fled a raging civil war. The husband asked me if I would like tea or coffee, and I eagerly said yes to a coffee. I waited outside the shop for a long time, and I wondered what was taking so long, but it turned out that it was the first cup of coffee they had made. It was the best coffee I'd had in a very long time.

Before I knew it, I had passed through Oxford, and the few hills I had encountered to that point were not too harsh but I did have to stop a good few times to catch my breath and rest. I was reluctant to push the bike up hills, because I had nerve damage to the whole of my right side, and quite often when I thought I'd lifted my right foot off the floor when walking, I hadn't. I'd go arse over tit, and the last place I'd want to land was in a live lane of traffic. I had fallen over so often that Sue couldn't help but laugh at times. She said it was incredible to watch such a big man floating to the ground like an autumn leaf. I was hardly anything like an "autumn leaf", but I learned over time to hit the floor as softly as I could to protect my spine. I would fall in ways that would give me the least amount of pain, much like a stuntman or martial artist would, but nowhere near as graceful. Sue once watched in horror as I rolled about 15 feet along a footbridge before she burst into laughter, and I ended up laughing with her.

I couldn't risk falling into live traffic if I stopped on the side of a hill, so each time I paused I tried to make sure I was leaning left, putting weight on my left foot. My right leg was also much weaker than my left, and the beauty of cycling was that my left leg helped to keep the right leg moving and took up the slack. I was also aware that when cycling on the right side of the road abroad, I would still have to lean on my left leg, and the thought of having to lean into the road instead of away from it concerned me a little. I hoped that, by then, I'd have learned a few tricks that would keep me out of harm's way.

The reason for the nerve damage was that, years before, I had worked for a facility management company, and I was part of a team installing a lane closure on the M6 in Birmingham. I'd heard a rumble behind me as I stood on the hard shoulder and turned my head in time to see the front of an articulated lorry, just before it struck me. I was lucky to survive, but ended up with spine and nerve damage. The driver accepted liability, but I was dismissed from my job on capability grounds as I could no longer carry out my duties as before. The accident had a considerable impact on not only my income at the time and physical health, but also my mental health in the form of PTSD and situational anxiety. However, it wasn't too long before I was back on my financial feet.

My health was a big reason I chose the Rohloff Speedhub for the bike. It was an internally geared hub, and I could set the gear I wanted by turning a twist shifter on the handlebars, and not have to turn the pedals like with a derailleur set-up. Getting nearly 500 pounds moving again on the side of a hill was relatively easy and, due to the hub, the spokes in the rear wheel were shorter, which added to the wheel's strength. The force that I put on the rear wheel and gearing, and the force on the whole of the bike from a standing start or hill start, must have been off the scale.

My size prevented me from standing to pedal if it got tough. I was concerned my weight, plus pulling down on the handlebars might snap or damage a pedal. I wondered how much damage I could do if I broke a pedal or my foot slipped off one and hit the floor. I couldn't take the chance.

And so, after yet another comfortable night in my tent, I was just 22 miles north of Woodstock, and awoke to another dull, rainy day. I packed up the soaking wet gear and headed out. I arrived at the campsite to find that tents weren't allowed. It was motorhomes and caravans only, so I offered to pay the motorhome pitch price but still no joy, so I headed to a hotel five miles away. Once booked in, I had a hot bath and washed some clothes before diving into lovely clean sheets.

The next morning there was a clicking noise, and I couldn't tell whether it was coming from the pedals or the rear wheel. I could also feel vibrations in my right foot, so I made a phone call to the dealership. We agreed the noise could have been parts settling in. I pottered along that morning, taking in the scenery, when all of a sudden I found myself getting off the road as fast as I could in panic. A truck had gone past me, and it had a loose trailer strap that swiped my arm. I managed to hold myself together as I darted off the road and took shelter out of the rain under a large oak tree. The situational anxiety I suffered was caused by being close to large vehicles as a pedestrian. The rumbling of wheels and the draught as they passed had me cringing.

My enlarged heart was pounding out of my chest as I stood staring out at the chaotic traffic. I focused on the road's two-foot shoulder I'd been riding on, and on how narrow the road was. Trucks flew past at high speed, and rainwater sprayed up into a dense mist. I seemed to focus in on every little thing, yet moments earlier, I had been riding along like I didn't have a care in the world. I knew cycling in traffic would be a massive challenge. I also knew I would have to fight that mental state and my physical limitations, so I gave myself a good talking to and continued.

At just over a week on the road, I was ready to take on my biggest range of hills: the Chiltern Hills. I found a campsite in Wallingford, and it was the perfect time to call into a bike shop to get some professionals to look at what all the clanging and grinding was. The noise had become so loud that people standing by the roadside would look to see what was coming. A bike built for world travel might not even get me out of the UK, I thought. The staff at the Rides On Air bike shop in the town got straight to work, stripping the pedals and cleaning out the bottom bracket. The reason they went for that area rather than the rear of the bike or the Speedhub was because I told them my dealership thought it was likely grit or sand in the bottom bracket. The staff found nothing wrong with the bottom bracket, but made me a great cup of coffee and didn't even charge for the work.

Back in my tent at Bridge Villa Camping and Caravan Park, I tried to plan my route through the hills. I was in the perfect spot to be able to cut through the Chilterns without any significant climbs.

Using navigation apps on my iPhone and Garmin Edge Explorer 1000 took some working out. The Garmin turned out to be a complete waste of money for me, so it just sat in the bottom of one of the pannier bags in case my phone packed in. I couldn't get used to it, and much preferred Google Maps and Maps.me. When people asked what route I was taking or how I mapped my route in advance, they'd be visibly shocked to hear I had no physical maps or any rigid plans at all. I would point south and say, "I'm going that way." The lack of solid route planning seemed a bit scary to some but, to me, it meant more adventure and a more significant challenge.

The shocked expressions regarding routes were nothing compared with facial contortions when they were made aware I hoped to cycle many countries. Some tried to hide their reactions, but most couldn't summon the strength to hold back from looking me up and down. I was sure I caught one person managing to scan me from head to toe with just one eye while maintaining eye contact with the other. Given my build, I must have looked a highly unlikely bicycle tourist.

The next morning, all seemed well as I cycled out of the campsite in the rain and onto a muddy farm track. It wasn't too long before I was on some tarmac and, six miles later in torrential rain, I found a café in Goring that served a full English breakfast. It was just what I needed to warm and cheer me up.

While I waited for my breakfast, a man with his son approached my table to ask about my adventure. He pointed at my bike and asked if I did any camping. I said, "Yes, I do." I looked over to the bike and pointed in the direction of where I had strapped my tent. To my horror, it wasn't there. I couldn't believe it as I dashed over to the bike to make sure.

Because the tent was wet that morning, I had strapped it to the rear rack underneath the rack-pack, in the hope the weather would brighten up and dry it out. The strap holding it had come off, and the tent had fallen off during the six miles to the café.

Just when I thought things couldn't get any worse, my breakfast was brought to the table. I didn't have time for breakfast; I had to find my tent before someone else did, so I grabbed the black pudding and bacon and started back towards the campsite.

I scanned the road ahead, including the hedgerows and ditches. I was eventually just a few hundred yards from the site, and I could see a red lump in the middle of the muddy track I had started the day on. It was my tent! I couldn't believe it. When setting out that morning, the farm track was bone-shaking, and I'd slipped a few times, ending up with the bike on its side. There was lots of thumping and banging as I rattled along the track, so I didn't notice the tent falling off and hitting the ground. After that mishap, I made sure always to loop the handles of the bag over the seat post.

At the point of finding my tent I had travelled 12 miles in the rain to get back to where I'd started, but I wasn't at all devastated: I was happy to find the tent. I then had to start heading back for my breakfast six miles away. A couple of miles later, the rain became so heavy that every car that passed created a wave that soaked me. I took cover in what looked like an old wooden bus shelter. I sat there soaking wet, feeling sorry for myself and trying to use my phone's touch-screen with wet, crinkly fingertips when a truck pulled up. The driver came over and asked if I was okay or in need of a lift. I must have looked a right sorry state as I sat there wondering if my fried bread had soaked up all the tomato juice and gone mushy. I told him about the café, and it turned out he was going the same way. I had no problem taking the lift because I'd already made the trip once, and back, and nearly halfway back again: a total of 14 miles of cycling, and I was starving.

We loaded the gear and set off back to the café, where I was horrified to find my breakfast had vanished. I explained my situation to the staff, but I got blank stares. I hadn't told them to keep it warm for me, so it was my fault they cleared it up. I didn't want to shell out on another one, so I kept going in the hope of finding a campsite in the afternoon.

The rain seemed to get worse, so I decided to book into the first guesthouse I came across, and what an excellent guesthouse it was. The lovely owners at the Weir View in Pangbourne gave me a significant discount because they probably felt a little sorry for me, as I must have looked like a drowned rat. They even put cardboard on the floor in their elegant kitchen so I had a place for the bike. I had a nice hot bath and dove into the fluffiest of beds, but not before a burger and chips at The Swan pub across the road.

After a hearty breakfast I was through the Chilterns, but the clicking noise on the bike was back. I called into the Pedal On bicycle shop in Tadly, where the staff made me a coffee and stripped out the bottom bracket, with no charge. I loved how caring some bike shop assistants were with me, and it was much appreciated. The noise had gone, and as I cycled in the direction of Portsmouth, I passed through wheat fields, over rivers, and past lakes and thatched cottages in tiny villages.

While riding my last big range of hills, the South Downs, I met some guys at Holden Farm Camping who were touring on motorbikes. We set up our tents close together and got a fire going after a few jars at a pub. I enjoyed the company, and we had a good laugh.

I was soon nearly at Portsmouth, where I had planned to catch a ferry to France, and I was feeling a little nervous. I contacted the dealership to express my concerns regarding the noise the bike was still making. I asked whether it would be a good idea to take it back up to the shop while I was still in the country. I was told not to worry, and that even if I had problems, there would be plenty of bike shops in France able to help.

I fought with myself as to whether to cross to France or not. I also started thinking I should've gone with a simpler set-up: cantilever brakes instead of discs, derailleur gears and chain instead of the Speedhub and carbon belt. That would have been a configuration most bike shops could work with almost anywhere in the world. I was also feeling a little nervous and sad about leaving loved ones for many months, or even a year or two. I wondered whether I was having second thoughts and looking for ways to blame the bike for ending my adventure.

So much had happened since leaving home, and in such a short time in miserable weather, that I wondered whether bicycle touring was actually my thing. Just two weeks in and my feelings were all over the place. I imagined that arriving in another country with my bike would be the actual start of the adventure, and I wouldn't be returning for some time. I had to decide what I wanted to do, as the ferry to France was leaving from Portsmouth the next day.

CHAPTER 2

It was surprising what a person can do

Looking back to Portsmouth from the deck of the Saint-Malo-bound ferry felt strange. I knew I had made the right decision to continue, and it was incredible to think I was about to cycle in another country. It was sunny and warm as I left the ferry and rode into France. My targets for the day were first to adapt to riding on the wrong side of the road, then cycle just seven miles to a campsite I had spotted online. On arrival, I had to beg with puppy dog eyes for the last available pitch. I only had the eyes of a very old bloodhound, but somehow they did the trick.

I set up the tent and took the opportunity to get all my clothes clean using the on-site washing machines. When I had everything hung on a washing line that I strung between a tree and a fence, my camping neighbours approached and invited me to their birthday barbeque. I thought it was kind of them and a great welcome to France. They were two young French couples who spoke a little English, so we were able to communicate and have a great afternoon. I then took a short ride to an estuary and sat on a bench to write my daily blog. As I hammered away at the laptop keyboard, a mother and daughter walked over from their house nearby and handed me a crepe. It was so lovely of them, and it was delicious. I didn't know what to expect from the French, as I had previously never met more than a handful in my life, but after that first day I had an excellent feeling.

After packing up on my second day in France, I decided to head south through Brittany towards Rennes, then on to the coastal city of Saint-Nazaire. Saint-Nazaire was a few days away, but I felt that, once on the coast, I'd find a lot of campsites with more available pitches.

Later that morning, while reading the map, I fell off the bike right into a bramble patch and it was hard work untangling myself and the bike. My first proper day in France wasn't going so well. I had managed to time my tour in France during a holiday period with barely any shops open, and I had just two bottles of water and a few chocolate bars when I set out. I was so sorry I hadn't placed an order for bread at the campsite the evening before.

The site manager had asked me if I wanted to order baguettes, but I'd thought it was quite a funny thing to ask so I declined. I had never heard of anyone requesting bread at a campsite, but I'd have snatched her hands off for a bacon butty.

I rode for 20 miles before I found a campsite, and it was great to see it had a fully functioning bar and restaurant. I was looking forward to tucking into a substantial meaty meal because a mixed grill was on the menu. Sadly, it wasn't a mixed grill by any stretch of the imagination. It had two skinny sausages, one thin slice of pressed ham, and a handful of toothpick-sized fries. I was sure I had burned more calories eating it than was in it! Due to all the cycling, food was always on my mind.

I pedalled like the clappers the next morning to a town I'd spotted on the map that appeared to have a lot of hotels and eateries. After 35 miles of small rollercoaster hills and well-maintained roads, I arrived with a huge appetite. I could have eaten a horse and jockey, though I thought the chance of a jockey being on the menu in France was slim. Sadly, the town seemed abandoned, and all that was missing was tumbleweed. I couldn't find a place to stay and had no choice but to carry on until I found something else.

A little while later, I cut through some farmland to shave off some miles and found myself in an area overgrown with tall grasses and all sorts of large shrubs. I spotted a couple of guys with large Doberman dogs a little farther up the narrow road I was on, and the dogs were going doolally for some reason. I didn't like the idea of cycling past such big, angry-looking dogs, so I checked the map and found a little track. No sooner was I on it than the sound of a shotgun rang out, and I nearly jumped out of my overstretched skin. I looked to the bushes and could see a man shouting and waving his arms in the air. He was wearing what looked like a cartoon duck-hunting hat and was holding a shotgun, and behind him were a few other guys with guns. The gaggle of Elmer Fudd-looking fellows were hunting and shooting critters in the bushes, and probably using the Dobermans to drive them out, or to collect them. I hadn't a clue what the men were hunting. I was more concerned with just getting out of there as quickly as I could with my head still on my shoulders.

As the day went on, it became clear I wouldn't make it to a campsite before dark, so I pulled into a picnic area right next to a road and sat at a table eating the morsels I had. I then locked my bike to a tree in the bushes and set up the tent in a small clearing a few yards from the picnic area. I later had a good chuckle to myself as I lay in my bag, reflecting on the day's events. I slept like a baby.

It was so hard to believe it had been 17 days since I left Cheshire, and even harder to think I had managed such a distance. In those 17 days I had learned that padded shorts were a must, although even with padded shorts, my butt was red-raw. I could only imagine what it would have been like without the padding. I had also learned that a lot of the muscle I had developed through years of weight training would prove useless when it came to cycling. My leg muscles were okay due to the heavy load they were pushing for hours each day. I had to accept I didn't need big biceps and shoulder muscles for cycling, and I couldn't be bothered to exercise them after a long day of cycling.

I learned the importance of carrying extra food and water in any available space. Even in built-up areas, buying healthy food and clean water wasn't always possible. I also never knew when I might have to wild camp, so it was essential to have a few small supplies to see me through a day or two. I had to try to relax and not be in so much of a rush. It was my nature to want things right away, and I'd get so frustrated when I could see something in my mind and not be able to get it or achieve it quickly.

There was just one more day of cycling to go before getting to the coast, and what a fabulous day it was. The weather conditions were perfect, and I overtook my first bicycle tourist who was at least half my age and weight. It was a great feeling to cycle alongside him for a few seconds to say hello, before I powered away into the distance. 'Powered away' may have been a slight exaggeration. I had been overtaken by other cyclists so many times that I just once wanted to know what it felt like to do the passing, and it felt great. Keeping my face straight, the sweat from my brow, and my knees from buckling took some doing though, and I kept looking back in my handlebar mirrors until the guy was out of sight. A few minutes later I spotted a supermarket and turned into the car park, where I nearly collapsed.

Well, I had no plans to go on an ego trip like that again; and for all I knew, the guy might have cycled 100 miles and been at death's door that day for me to pass him as I did.

The supermarket was just what I needed. I filled all available spaces in my bags with as much small, high-calorie food as I could, then I managed to locate a campsite nearby. Almost £20 for a campsite pitch! I nearly died, though it did look good, and I did need a shower. I was surprised to find the price also included a washing machine token and the rental of an electrical extension cable and free power supply to my tent. The internet speed was good on-site too, so I downloaded and watched a movie on my laptop. I chose a computer with a Solid State Drive (SSD) because it had no moving parts. A Hard Disk Drive (HDD) would likely not have survived my time in the UK, as the bumps and bangs and the bike falling over on tracks would have had it falling apart. I also carried an external SSD drive to back up files.

Charging all the electronics was not always easy. The SON dynamo built into the front wheel had two USB sockets and should have been a good idea. It proved to be a colossal waste of money though, because I needed to maintain a good pace consistently to get just a little charge on my phone, which I couldn't do. I wasn't quick, and I'd also have to stop a lot on hills or when I ran out of breath or to check the map. It only came in handy when in low light or tunnels to power the lights. The two EasyAcc 20000mAh power banks I had were light and compact. They were a reliable way of keeping my electronics charged throughout the day, and doubled as torches. I would get nearly a week out of them when fully charged, and I had no problem asking campsite reception staff to plug them in or charge them for me overnight.

Heading to the coast the following morning felt great, and the Saint-Nazaire Bridge loomed large in the distance. After a nice ride with the wind to my back I arrived at the bridge, but couldn't figure out how to get on it. While I was looking at the map, a guy pulled up in his car and asked if I needed help. I told him I wanted to get across the bridge, so he suggested I followed his car, and in no time at all I was pedalling over the bridge. He had kindly offered to buy me lunch before I crossed the bridge, but I was in a bit of a rush to reach a campsite before dark. The bridge wasn't anywhere near as hard going as it looked from a distance. However, lots of campervan drivers got far too close as I rode a very narrow cycle strip, and a few had my nerves gone. From the top of the bridge, I could see what seemed days of cycling ahead down the coast. There was a strong wind as I crossed the bridge, but I flew down the other side.

I was thrilled I'd made it to the seaside town of Pornic. The place was buzzing, and there was a fireworks display scheduled for that evening. Police and soldiers lined the roads and stood at roadblocks with machine guns, taking no chances due to some recent terrorist attacks in France. The theme of the fireworks display was a battle between the French and British. The French won, of course. I was in France, after all. I had a great evening and plenty to eat and drink, and I loved being on the coast. I liked the sounds of the ocean, and the seaside smells, and there was often plenty going on.

The next night, at another campsite, I set up my tent next to a large motorhome that was owned by a circus clown. He didn't speak any English, so he communicated with me the best way he could - by offering me a beer. It was my kind of communication. There was also a young family who were camping to the other side of me, and they invited me to eat some food with them, which I gratefully accepted. They also insisted I had a coffee with them the following morning.

I left the campsite with the wind to my back, and soon found myself in a marshland known as the Marais Poitevin, also referred to as Green Venice. Riding through the stunning marshes was enjoyable and, after a short while, a car came alongside me. The lady driver asked if I wanted a drink and some lunch at her house. She said it was just up the road and her husband would be cool with it. The house was lovely, and the owners said I could have a shower if I needed to freshen up. I had only been on the road a few hours, so although it was kind of them to offer, I skipped the shower and dived headfirst into the salmon pâté crackers and beer on the table. I loved meeting such friendly, helpful people; it always made my day.

I enjoyed the coastline to La Rochelle, and it was time to visit the local KOGA dealership there to get things sorted. After finding a cheap central campsite and dumping my gear in the tent, I took a short ride to the dealership to find out what the bike's grinding noise and vibrations were due to. I had paid a lot of money for the bike, and I expected excellent service, but that wasn't what I got from Holland Bikes in La Rochelle.

I cycled to the shop feeling great, because I thought the noise was going to get fixed. On arrival, I told an assistant that the bike was only a few months old and still under warranty and it had a problem. I instantly got the feeling he didn't want to know, and I hadn't even gone into detail at that point. I thought his response was stone cold, and I started to get a little worked up as I explained the issue. The assistant went over to the bike and turned the pedals backwards. His eyes went straight to the Rohloff Speedhub as he listened to the grinding, and my heart sank. The staff thought that tiny metal filings might have been inside the hub, causing the grinding noise and meaning an oil change was needed to clean it out. The assistant asked me to call back to the shop a few days later with the bike while they got an oil kit sent over. I told him I was living in a tent and I would call back the following day to see if they had an oil kit delivery date.

The hub was like the gearbox of a car, with all the cogs being inside a casing. A syringe was needed to extract the old oil and insert new. I returned to my tent, then a little later on I went and sat at a lovely harbour bar and had beer and pizza, after an excellent but expensive haircut. While I sat soaking up stunning views, I thought about the life I'd lived.

It had been a fascinating and enjoyable life for the most part. I had travelled all over the world, loved and loved some more, married twice, and fathered two daughters. I'd worked hard for every little thing I'd done or had, and I had experienced things many would have found hard to believe or imagine. I had befriended people from all walks of life and many different races, genders and cultures. I had lived my life my way, with a philosophy of shit or bust, all or nothing, and I put everything I had into everything I did. Not everything worked out - far from it – but I was never one for giving up. No matter what was going on in my life, I always managed a big smile and tried to help anyone who needed help.

Before writing this book, I had only ever told my wife Sue about what happened to me as a child, and I didn't share it until I'd turned fifty. It was something I didn't think I could share before that, not with my sisters or anyone else. As a child, I'd had the worst kind of father a child could have: a monster, a predator. I was unruly back then, and I later put that mostly down to what I went through, although there was a good chance I would have still been a little shit. I often ran away from home, only to end up petrified and lonely in the dark of the Australian bush, or shivering in cardboard or wrapped up in roofing insulation in houses that were under construction. I even tried to sleep in a cardboard box in the middle of the city of Perth when I was just 12 years old. I was rarely away for long and would return to face the not-so-pleasant music. There was food at home and a bed, and my mum and three wonderful sisters.

I found it hard to concentrate at school and always wanted to be somewhere else; like most children, no doubt. But I wouldn't only want to be somewhere else; I'd be somewhere else in my mind. I had the cane more times than anyone in the entire school, and my slightly younger sister Sue would often hear my name called over the classroom speakers. She told me she knew I was in trouble and often felt sad. We were close to the same age and like buddies a lot of time, and would often hang around together and get up to mischief. However, my sisters were also having a terrible time.

I'd often pretend to go to school and then make my way to the bush or river nearby to look for snakes and other critters. Some snakes I caught were deadly poisonous, but I didn't care. I captured all sorts of things, and mum got a bit annoyed when I sometimes took critters home. I liked to be around the wildlife and out in the open air. The bush was a place to escape; I loved being on my own at times, but not all the time. I felt the same way as an adult, which didn't help relationships run too smoothly because it seemed to some that I was always running away.

I slept well at the campsite in La Rochelle, feeling that at least the problem with the bike had been located and would soon be fixed. The next morning after breakfast, I spent an hour fruitlessly fishing in the harbour with tackle I had brought from home, which consisted of a spinning rod and reel and a few lures. I then made my way back to the bike shop, where I was received with a smirk and a shrug from the very rude assistant when I asked when the oil kit would arrive. I stared at him for what seemed like minutes, as my blood began to boil. He then turned around and started working on some boxes before I got his attention.

The guy must have sensed that I was about to unleash on him, because he pointed to the phone and slowly reached for it. It was as though he was trying not to spook me into doing something silly. He spoke to a woman on the phone then handed the phone over to me. The woman told me it wasn't their problem because the Rohloff Speedhub was not a KOGA part. She made it clear that only KOGA parts, such as the frame and the handlebars were covered and not the whole bike. I tried to keep my cool and told her I had thousands of followers across my social media platforms.

I also told her the ride was also in support of a children's charity. I figured it was at least worth a shot, and it was true anyway. She then asked me to hand the phone back to the assistant, and she asked him to take down the serial number for her. A little while later there was a lot of commotion, and other members of staff came out and started looking at the bike.

I kept my dealer at Cyclesense in the UK fully informed about what was going on while I sat on a bench outside the shop, and to his credit he told me he had been in contact with KOGA about it. Holland Bikes and I were sent instructions by email on how to apply thick grease to stop the "operational noise" from the hub's splined carrier. It turned out other cyclists who had bought the hub and carbon drive belt instead of a chain had reported noises. I had doubts the problem I was experiencing was just noise. To me, it seemed like something was viciously wearing away. A slight noise would have been no problem. The shop applied some grease to help keep the noise down and gave me a bill for €95, about £80 at the time, which they said I had to claim from my dealer in the UK.

My dealer deposited the money to my bank straight away, even though he had nothing to do with the La Rochelle bike shop. He also apologised to me for the poor treatment I had received in La Rochelle. Without assistance from my dealer, I would have probably been in a bit of a mess. After being treated so well by Cyclesense, Pedal On, and Rides On Air back in the UK, the terrible treatment I received in La Rochelle came as a real shock. I usually felt a little alone when I had problems far from home, because it was all down to me to sort them out. But because I had done a lot of travelling on my own and had created businesses over the years, I had become quite a good problem solver. I often thought it was surprising what a person can do when only that person can.

Despite the bike and shop problems, La Rochelle was great, and I loved some of the graffiti in the area. I told myself I would return someday as a regular tourist to spend time enjoying the bars and restaurants and stunning buildings. A few beers on my last night in La Rochelle to wash down a great meal had set me up with the calories and mood to continue down the coast the next morning.

During the next 35 miles to a campsite in what felt like 100-degree heat, I called into a supermarket that sold fresh, cold milk, which I often found challenging to locate in France. Although most shops and supermarkets sold long-life or vegan and vegetarian types, it appeared to me that few people liked pasteurised. I couldn't get enough of it.

Arriving at Campsite Valerick in Saint-Sornin was a relief. I was hot and shattered and ready for a cold shower and some clean clothes. The campsite wasn't rated very highly, but it was one of the nicest I'd come across. It had clean showers, well-maintained grounds, and it was quiet, with a fast internet connection. I concluded that small, family-run, lower-rated campsites were perfect. Some of the highly-rated campsites had been terrible. They were possibly only top-rated because they might have had an unmaintained tennis court or toad-filled swimming pool.

I awoke refreshed, then made my way to the seaside town of Royan, where I sat at a lovely bar drinking a cold beer while working out how much farther I had to cycle to reach Spain. It was just 200 miles. Although 200 miles didn't sound much of a distance compared with what I'd already done in a month, it was still a good few days away for me.

Later in the day I found a campsite on a hill next to a great beach, where I hurried to erect my tent on a patch of soft sand next to a wooden picket fence. There was a storm coming, and I was hoping for a swim before it arrived. I had the most fantastic view from the tent and could see the angry-looking storm clouds approaching, so I made my way down the hill and dived into the Atlantic Ocean. Once in the water, I stripped off completely, as the only other person in the water that I could see was at least 400 yards away, and with my last bar of soap I scrubbed the grime out of my clothes.

That night, the storm hit hard, thumping at my tent, and I could hear all kinds of things being thrown about outside. I could only hope none of those flying objects would go through my tent. I lay awake for what must have been five minutes, as usual, before I fell fast asleep, waking only to the loudest thunderclaps. I had learned to use sounds in the night to help me to sleep, like the rustling of leaves and creaking branches, crickets, frogs and other critters, even passing vehicles. Barking dogs were a nightmare.

As I crawled out of my tent in the morning, there was debris everywhere from the storm. After a wash, I packed up and headed towards the Dune of Pilat, which was said to be the tallest sand dune in Europe.

A little later that morning I found myself among a group of bicycle tourists who were heading in the same direction, but only riding down the coast to Spain. They were doing about 50 miles a day, every day, which was more than I was covering. I tagged myself to the end of the group and did my best to keep up, and I started chatting with a few of them. They were heading to catch a ferry across an inlet, then cycle down to the famous dune. We cycled 22 miles in what seemed no time at all, pushing each other along, chatting and having a giggle. It was great to have company, and the miles flew by. One of the guys had a tricycle, another had a battery-assisted bike, and all of them were travelling super light. They had pre-planned their route and booked into hotels, bed and breakfasts and guesthouses in advance, so they didn't have to carry anywhere near as much equipment and clothing as I did. I thought it must have been bliss.

We all had lunch together while waiting for the ferry to the town of Arcachon, and the guys had a healthy lunch of sardines and salad, while I had two pints of beer. I'd already had a fair amount of food for breakfast and wasn't hungry. They said they didn't like to drink beer during their ride because it sapped energy. I hadn't given that a thought, but I rarely drank beer if I was still planning to cycle. I much preferred it as a treat in an evening.

After disembarking the ferry, we cycled a few more miles together then parted ways on a small-but-steep hill that the tricycle rider and I struggled on. The guy with the electric-assist bike flew up it like a rat up a drainpipe. It was quite sad to say goodbye as I'd enjoyed having the company, and I felt alone as soon as we parted. It made me think how much more fun and more relaxed it would have been if I had cycled with another person or group, but that wouldn't have been the challenge I wanted. I made my way to a campsite at the base of the dune. I was far too tired to climb it like every other camper seemed to be doing. So I carried out my usual washing and tent-erecting routine and tucked myself up in my bag.

I had always been a big protein eater, and I was finding it hard to get the protein I felt my body needed. I could have eaten some sardines with the guys, but I had never liked fresh sardines, and those slippery little suckers were not the food I was craving. I made it a mission, the day of leaving the dune, to find a slab of hard cheese, a whole cooked chicken, and a couple of pints of cold, whole milk.

I arrived in a small town, and my eyes nearly fell out of my weather-beaten skull. There it was, like a light at the end of a very long tunnel - a shop selling whole, cooked chickens! I couldn't believe it. I was soon at the front of the queue, waiting patiently until the shopkeeper looked straight past me to the person behind and started talking in French. I was in France, after all. He appeared to be asking what the person behind me wanted, so I moved my head between them and said to the shopkeeper, "HELLO, it's me; I'm next."

The shopkeeper opened a large book on the table and asked my name. I said my name wasn't in the book, so he shut it with a loud and almost dusty thud. He then took a step back and crossed his arms out in front of him, to make an X, suggesting that because I hadn't pre-ordered, I wasn't getting a chicken. Well, my jaw nearly hit the floor, and I said in a bit of a harsh tone, "You're kidding me; please sell me a chicken."

My tone wasn't great, I knew that, but the sight of those delicious-looking chickens going around and around in the rotisserie for the 20 minutes as I stood in the queue was hypnotic, and I reacted. I was just a bit down about it and turned into a giant baby. I ended that day with a pathetic-looking bowl of seafood pasta from a small stall. As I looked at the meagre offering, it appeared to be nothing more than a scattering of empty seashells scraped from a crappy beach, with a single, sorry-looking shrimp on the top. I then started laughing out loud, because I couldn't believe I had been so silly over food.

I had made it to just 60 miles from the border to Spain. But if there was one thing I'd learned when it came to mapping distances, it was that I was always way out. Thankfully, I was in no rush, and having no road route planned before each day added a bit of adventure and interest.

I also found a fancy supermarket, with high prices but worth it due to the quality of the foods I'd been craving. I sat on the floor of the supermarket car park with about ten pounds of protein between my legs: £16 for a whole chicken, a lump of cheese I could ski jump-off, and four pints of icy-cold milk. I wanted to pinch myself, but my skin had stopped snapping back days earlier. I sat there on the floor until all but two pints of milk and a small chunk of mauled cheese were left. I could hardly breathe, and it felt great.

The next day I awoke with so much energy I felt like I could have cycled all day without stopping until I reached the border. By evening and just 18 miles shy, my tank was empty. I found a campsite and set up the tent as quickly as I could so that I could fall asleep looking forward to crossing the border in the morning.

CHAPTER 3

Couldn't get through, but I wasn't one to give up

Arriving in Spain, I expected a physical border crossing and some checks, or at least something that would let me know I was about to cross a border. There was nothing that I could see on the minor road I cycled down into Irun. I located a crappy and expensive campsite just five miles north of San Sebastian, where I met a couple who were travelling in a motorhome. They invited me over to share some wine and have a chat, and I went to bed a little sloshed, but awoke excited and looking forward to what Spain had to offer. I had cycled through England and along the Atlantic Coast of France, and I was now in Spain. Not bad at all for my first bicycle tour, I thought. My daughters expressed how proud they were of their dear old dad by uploading posts to their social media about the distance I'd covered.

The reason I chose to camp five miles from San Sebastian was that my intention wasn't to spend too long in the city. It was to take a few photographs and cycle on in the direction of Bilbao, roughly 70 miles farther along the coast. From Bilbao, I planned to head inland to Madrid, before heading from Madrid to Valencia. The distance from San Sebastian to Valencia was roughly 600 miles, and I estimated it could take me at least two weeks, maybe longer.

I thought San Sebastian was stunning, and there happened to be a large sailing regatta that day. The city was heaving with tourists, but I managed to fight my way through to a beach area to take some photos. A couple of guys came over to chat, and they invited me to stay at an apartment they were renting nearby, which was kind of them. It was still very early in the day, and I wanted to keep moving. As I cycled out of San Sebastian, I looked to the Basque Country hills and snow-capped mountains in the distance, and for some strange reason, I felt a pull towards them. I decided to forget about cycling along the coast to Bilbao and, instead, cycle straight through that glorious but lumpy landscape, all the way to Madrid. The freedom to choose the direction I wanted to go on a whim felt just how I'd imagined it would: fantastic.

I picked a point on the map I felt I could reach that day, and it was the town of Tolosa, just 20 miles away. I could easily do that, I thought, regardless of how hilly it was. After a few miles of metal fencing and all manner of obstacles, I met a lovely local family who filled my bottles with cold water. They told me the route I had in mind was blocked, and that I would have to check my maps and come up with another plan. I thanked them for the water and set out to work around the closures as best I could.

I went up and down some steep hills, but at least I was on tarmac roads for the most part. It wasn't too long before I realised I had taken my bicycle helmet off when talking with the family earlier on and placed it on the rack-pack. It had fallen off at some point, and there was no way I was going back for it. I just kept going with a plan to pick up another helmet at the nearest bike shop. After hours of hard cycling, I ended up retreating to only one mile from where I'd started in San Sebastian. I felt destroyed, and all the excitement of just heading through the hills to Madrid had gone. I couldn't get through that time but I wasn't one to give up, so I sat on a step at a petrol station and started plotting.

I loaded up with food and water from the petrol station, just in case the next assault on the hills had me cycling late into the night which would have meant pitching the tent in the woods somewhere. I always did my best to avoid cycling in the dark, even with great lights and a high-visibility vest.

The petrol station attendants had been looking at me since I arrived, and they didn't like me being there. At one point they asked me to go, but I told them I had just spent a fortune inside and I would go when I was ready. Once ready, I stuck a couple of fingers up at the attendants. I then waited for a minute to see if they were going to do anything about it.

I stood there giving them a milk-curdling look, hoping it would put them off rushing me and beating me to a pulp, or at least having a go. As I cycled off, I looked towards the hills and shouted, "COME ON, LET'S HAVE IT," as I tried to psych myself up for the attack.

I eventually made it through, and the sun was about to set as I cycled into Tolosa, which seemed like a sort of rustic working town, and it had a beautiful fast-flowing river running through the middle. I put in the extra effort to keep going, and it paid off, but I needed to find somewhere to sleep and there were no campsites in the area I could find. However, I did manage to locate a hostel right in the centre.

I had never stayed in a hostel before. It was tatty looking on the outside, so I locked the bike to some stairs in the stairwell. I then went up to the reception, where the manager told me I needed a Pilgrim's Passport, otherwise known as a Credential if I wanted to stay the night. He told me I could usually apply for a Credential at the local church, but that it wasn't open for a couple of days. I put on a sad face and deflated myself right down to the size of an average-sized person, and it worked. He then told me that, due to my not having anywhere to sleep, he could photocopy my regular passport. I was given a private room with a window overlooking the river and town for £15 a night, so I booked two nights. I was happy to have a comfy place to chill and to give my gear and bags a sort out.

Not one of the stories I had read before starting my adventure could remotely compare with my own. I seemed to have been going through all kinds of problems and painful adjustments. At the same time, exciting and fantastical things were happening, almost daily.

After a quick shower and shave, I put on a clean, dry change of clothes, opened my great little collapsible umbrella, and made my way in the rain to one of the many small local tapas bars. I had never been to one, and couldn't remember ever having tapas, so I thought it would be interesting. I entered a large courtyard surrounded by small bars. Nothing special or posh looking, but they did seem relaxed and cosy. I perched myself on a tall stool against a bar as the rain hammered the courtyard outside and dozens of flies circled my head like vultures over a rotting carcass. The flies put me off trying the small plates of uncovered tapas that sat on the bar, and I instead settled for a packet of corn chips and a large draught lager for just £2.

The next day was dull and wet, but as I had planned to stay two nights, I decided to wash every item of clothing that I wanted to keep. There was a launderette across the road from the hostel that was simple enough to use, and soap powder was included in the cost and automatically added. All I had to do was put the washing in the dryers after the wash. A dark wash and a coloured wash went in and out in no time. It was also the perfect time to go through all my bags and have the big sort-out I had kept promising myself. I emptied the lot on the bed and all over the floor, then cleaned the bags with a wet cloth.

While taking a breather, I stood leaning on the windowsill, looking out to the river. I was surprised to see the manager walking across the flat roof of the floor below that had plant pots and a washing line stretched across it. He had two cans of beer and a bag of beer nuts, my favourite kind. He leaned into the window space, and we chatted for about half an hour about pretty much everything. It was then back to work sorting through the gear.

I wanted to create some order, but to also lighten the load and free up some space. I started with the front right repair and medical bag. I kept valuable items in the front panniers and the handlebar bag so that if a bag fell off, I would see it and be able to react instantly. I would kick the rear panniers from time to time with my heel if I heard a noise from the rear, just to make sure I could feel they were still attached. There were so many items in the medical and repair bag, but I managed to free up some space by getting rid of all the cardboard packaging. I had 480 sachets of testosterone gel, enough to last me at least through Europe. I would have been in trouble without the gel. Testosterone Replacement Therapy, or TRT, was prescribed by hospital specialists after my accident with the articulated lorry, to help strengthen and slow the deterioration of my spine, muscles and joints.

There was also a lot of packaging around my thyroid medication, asthma inhalers, painkillers and a few other medicines, as well as cardboard around spare inner tubes and an extra carbon drive belt. After emptying all the items into zip-lock plastic bags and packing things more neatly, I managed to free up about a third more space. I wasn't able to free a lot of space in the electronics bag, but I managed to organise it better. I then set about dealing with the rear panniers. I didn't have to do anything with the rack-pack, as it contained camping gear and I knew already it was nice and neat, with a little extra space available for food and water. The most room was in the two rear panniers. Clothes I hadn't worn and felt I wouldn't wear went into a rubbish bag. Because the quality of my clothing was so poor, the cost of posting them home would have been more than the value, even if I'd used a stamp.

With that big job done, I took the rubbish bag for a walk to some waste skips I could see across the bridge from the hostel. I thought before washing the clothes about what was worth cleaning and what was going in the skip. I estimated I must have freed up about ten pounds in weight and created enough free space to pack a turkey and a small jar of cranberry sauce. If only!

I went for a short walk to the river the next morning before setting out, and there were large trout basking on the surface. I was sure some were more than two feet long. I asked a local man why nobody was fishing. He told me there was a lot of pollution in the water from the factories and industry that ran the length of the Oria. Nobody wanted to fish for them if they couldn't eat them. He said tourists came to fish for them but let them go. It was a real shame to hear about the level of pollution.

Cycling out of town I felt the difference in weight instantly, though I soon filled the new spaces with water and food. At least the bags were filled with things I would use.

Later in the day, I managed to buy a new helmet in a town called Beasain, before hitting an extensive series of steep switchbacks. They took me so high up that I could see for miles across the most beautiful hills and valleys of Basque Country. At the top, there was a bar where I appeared to be the only customer. I had myself a nice, cold pint of lager and sat on a bench looking out across a beautiful valley lined with pine trees. It was then time to enjoy a bit of freewheeling down the other side.

I hadn't passed any campsites that day, and all the land seemed to be fenced off. Layers of barbed wire surrounded some patches of land and forest, and all the great-looking wild camping spots appeared owned and well protected, so I got out my phone and made an online booking into a cheap hotel in Alsasua-Altsasu.

When I arrived at the hotel I found it had no reception area, and the entrance door was locked. I had to ring a telephone number written on a board, but at least the message was written in English and Spanish. I called the number and received instructions and was soon in my room. It was cosy and very modern, with a double bed and white bedding, and it also had a large bathroom. I was happy to be in a warm, clean hotel out of the rain. I was also able to take the bike to the room.

After a shower, I went for a wander with my stretchy string shopping bag in the hope of finding a small supermarket or shop. I covered most of the town, always being directed by locals to a different shop, and each time, it was closed when I got there. I eventually stumbled on a small and nearly empty store that was just about to pull down the shutters. I dashed in and filled my bag with what I was familiar with: potato chips, bananas, bread rolls, and milk. I then returned to my hotel, which I approached from a different direction than the direction I had left the hotel. I was shocked to see a supermarket closing at the side of the hotel. I couldn't believe it. It was almost funny.

I found a great wild camping spot the following night. My skinny sleeping bag and an inflatable mattress two inches thick were a stark contrast to the sprung and crisp sheets, bathroom and toilet of the hotel.

In case I needed to use the loo when wild camping, I kept the two bicycle water bottles in my tent, next to the exit. One bottle, to the left of the door, contained drinking water. The other, to the right, was for peeing in. The tent had two openings, so after peeing, I would unzip the door on the downhill side, if there was one, and quickly empty the contents onto the ground. If there were no downhills I'd splurge it out in any direction, but away from where I had to walk. Most mornings, I would give the bottle a rinse out with some clean water if I had any, then give it a proper wash at the next opportunity. Peeing was quite straightforward, but for anything else I would have to be more imaginative, and I refused to use the bottles.

I set out again with more than 40 miles to cycle to reach a campsite, which wasn't a vast distance to cycle, but I was missing loved ones in a big way and feeling quite lonely and tired. I was missing a little bit of company, someone to chat with, and the crappy campsite I ended up at didn't help much either. It had dirty showers and far too many flies. It was one of the worst sites I had ever experienced. As usual, I soon snapped out of my mini-low and thought myself thankful for everything I had and what I was able to do, and I slept right through.

I was getting closer to Madrid and couldn't wait to reach it. I felt that making it there would be a massive achievement for me. After some small hills and a few gravel tracks the next day, which was dry, hot and sunny, I found a fantastic wild camping spot next to a mobile phone antenna. The antenna was on a large mound which had a rocky trail spiralling around it to the top. I had no idea what level of radiation phone antennae gave off, or whether they were harmful at all. I pushed the bike up the track to the top, and my rewards were that I still had most of my hair, and I also had a spectacular 360-degree view of beautiful farmland as far as I could see.

It was a great spot, but it was only mid-afternoon and flies were driving me nuts. There was no way I was going to spend the whole afternoon and night hiding in my tent from the flies. I decided to move on, and on, and on, as I struggled to find another wild camping spot. That situation was pretty typical. I would often find the best wild camping spots early in the day when it was much too early to camp, so I would move on, then struggle to find anything else later.

The sun wasn't far off setting when I spotted an abandoned piggery with no roof, but walls that looked quite stable from a distance. I walked inside and across broken glass, and the stench of shit was so thick in the air, I could have almost cut it with a knife. As I walked between the piles of human crap on the floor, I wondered how many people had used the building as a public toilet, besides me.

Suddenly the wind picked up, and the unsupported walls that had looked firm from a distance started to sway. I couldn't risk the walls crashing down and flattening me in my tent in the night, and the stench was too much anyway so I pressed on.

I was 20 miles away from the next town, and it was late, and I was tired. I didn't know if I could make it before dark, or even if I would find a place to stay when I got there. I thought if I kept going, I might find a place to wild camp at some point, so I pushed on, and just five miles later I came across a campsite. I couldn't believe it. It was an excellent site with a bar and restaurant. After settling in, I went over to the bar, where I was the only patron. I ordered a beer and a pizza with everything on it, which may not have been the best idea, due to not having a clue what their version of "everything" was, but I was too hungry to care. I was also too hungry to care about the myriad flies zipping into the kitchen and not coming back out.

The next morning, I was itching to get going, so I had a quick wash and applied and consumed my meds, and I was on the road for sun-up. I managed 48 miles that day through some incredible countryside that reminded me of the Wild West. It was a complete contrast to the hills I had passed through, where everything looked deep green and fertile. Within just a few days of being in the Basque Country hills, the terrain had turned dry and dusty, and the ground gently undulated. Small towns and villages I came across reminded me of the Wild West movies I had watched growing up. Many Spaghetti Westerns were produced in Spain due to the landscape, though they should have been called Paella Westerns.

That night, just before dark, I waited for a tractor driver to finish turning a field in the distance before I darted into a small wood to set up my tent and gear-shed to hide the bike. I was in stealth mode due to being in a small patch of woodland surrounded by freshly cultivated fields. I was confident my green tent deep in the bushes was out of sight, and I made sure not to put any lights on in the night.

As I lay in my bag listening to dogs barking nearby, I got to thinking about wildlife in the area. I had read about wild boar being a bit of a pest and had even heard of brown bears and wolves in parts of Spain, but from what I understood, brown bears lived in the hills and mountains. Every time a twig snapped, I would sit up and try to listen to what might be out there. I wasn't scared, just curious, but I had a small flick-style knife at the ready in case a boar or other critter fancied its chances. I had plenty of supplies that night, including two pints of milk, a small shrink-wrapped chicken and a large loaf of bread - food I had picked up from a small shop that morning as I set out. I'd have fought any animal to the death over a cooked chicken! After all, I was on the verge of destroying a small town back in France over a chicken. As soon as my head hit the inflatable pillow I was out, and I had a great sleep, which I needed for the long, hot day ahead.

I liked getting an early start when the weather was great. I wanted to be gone that day super early in case the farmer returned. It was the first time I'd used my dynamo lights in the dark, and there was no traffic at all on the road. It felt quite spooky. I hoped to find a suitable campsite or hotel that day, as my clothes and I needed a good wash, and I had to charge the battery banks and laptop. I came off the road later in the morning and followed a gravel track, and I wondered if it was part of the network of Camino Trails. The route took me through small canyons carved by small streams, and I stopped at one point to ask two older women if they needed any water. I said, "Agua," while pointing to my bike bottles, but they just smiled and said they didn't need any water. I thought they might have been on a pilgrimage.

I got back on the road for a while and found a small picnic area, so it was time to eat the chicken. I flattened it out with the bones still inside, then slapped the whole thing between two halves of the loaf of bread. I did it for a photograph, as I thought it would be funny to post to social media later that day. The crazy things I did to amuse myself, I thought. I then removed the bones from the chicken and ate the whole thing with all the bread.

It was hot, and as I continued on the trails, tracks, and the odd bit of road in 100-degree heat, I ran out of water. I could see on the map a cluster of houses or buildings on my route, but I was unable to find shops. I came across a large warehouse with a couple of older men standing in the doorway, so I pulled in and pointed at my bottles on the bike. I said, "Hi, agua," and they responded instantly and gave me two large bottles of ice-cold water. One of the men looked at my bike and grabbed the bicep on my right arm, and we all started laughing. It was the people in small villages and places out of the way that made Spain feel special to me.

Later that day, I got lucky and came across a campsite. I bedded down after a proper cleansing in a shower block that needed a proper cleansing itself. When I'd lived in Western Australia flies were always a pain in the arse, and it seemed just the same north of Madrid. While cycling, I'd have only a few flies bothering me, but as soon as I stopped to check maps or have a rest, all the flies that must have been drooling over me as I passed had a chance to catch up, and some types were real biters. Getting inside my tent at the end of the day was my only escape, and it was no different at the campsite that day. I'd bought some fly spray when I purchased the food earlier, so I was able to zap a couple of flies that had made it into the tent.

I was so looking forward to Madrid, but I was gaining on the Sierra de Guadarrama mountain range. It was a bit of a surprise at first. I had expected a few lumps and bumps after Basque Country, but I didn't imagine a mountain range so close to Madrid.

I located the town of Riaza, and it had what looked like a large campsite and restaurant, so I made it my target. On the day I was due to arrive, a small tarmac and gravel road I had been riding on came to an abrupt end by leading onto a busy highway. I couldn't find any way to continue without getting on it. The signs on the on-ramp suggested no access for bicycles, so I gave it some serious thought while watching the speed of the traffic and some erratic drivers. I checked the maps and worked out that if I went on the highway, I would have a long way to cycle before I could get off, and I would be putting my life at risk.

I fought with myself for some time before deciding, like a fool, to go for it. I went down the on-ramp cycling like the clappers, dodging glass and bits of vehicle wreckage as I went. I then hugged the barrier so closely that I often hit it with my panniers. I could only hope I wouldn't get a puncture or get pulled by the fuzz. I was also getting a lot of justified abuse from people in vehicles. A few were hanging out of their windows shouting and telling me to get off, or words to that effect, which I couldn't wait to do. Some were only trying to help. I would have been horrified to see someone riding a bicycle along the hard shoulder of a major highway or motorway in the UK.

I wore my high-visibility vest with "Polite Think Bike" written on the back, which of course could look like "Police Think Bike" from a distance. I would usually wear the vest in heavy traffic or on roads that had no shoulder, in dim light or through city centres; otherwise, I wouldn't bother. I would wear my helmet in the same situations and on steep downhill roads, where I could reach high speeds. The relief I felt when leaving the highway was off the scale. I then had to push my bike up the steepest of gravel tracks for roughly half an hour, while flies were on me like I was the last turd on earth.

Shortly before arriving in Riaza, I stood at the side of the road straddling the bike, looking at my phone. I felt myself sliding sideways as the strange rusty red gravel I was on started to give way. I was slipping into a ditch that must have been ten feet deep so I fought to keep my balance, but fell into the road. Luckily, no vehicles were passing. I thought it was funny that I hadn't once fallen off my bike while moving, but I was sure there was time for that. Somehow, I managed to survive the day and make it to Camping Riaza.

After setting up my tent, I put my clothes, including all of my padded shorts, in the site's washing machine. I then realised what I had thought was a dryer was another washing machine, and I had no way of drying the clothes before morning. I thought my whole tour would have made a hilarious comedy. The site manager then told me the staff that ran the restaurant were on holiday. I started laughing and said to him that I should have guessed. I left my gear in the tent and rode into town, which was just up the road from the campsite. I found a great little cake shop, Trigo Limpio, where I had a tasty cheese and ham sandwich and a hot chocolate, then another cheese and ham sandwich.

I set out that next morning with a plan to attack the mountains with everything I had, and then ride the hilly terrain on the other side for a day or so down to Madrid. There was a major highway cutting through the mountains, and it was tempting. But I thought it would be safer for me to take some smaller roads I had located farther along the base of the range that then went up in a series of switchbacks. Well, that was the plan.

The day started well, with good roads, bad roads, and goats blocking my way. Not long into my ride, I began to climb steadily up the side of the range, and just as I was nearing the highest point on the road, I came across roadworks, and I couldn't get through. I could have cried. By the time I got back to the bottom, I had used up the best part of the day. I was also running low on food, water, and energy, so I decided the best thing to do was to get back to the campsite in Riaza. After nearly 30 miles of cycling in scorching heat and up the side of the range, I arrived back at the campsite with my tail between my legs.

I met a guy named Derek at the campsite, who was touring in a moto-rhome with his wife. We had a good chat, and the following morning they were parked at the campsite exit watching me as I lined myself up on the road and set out. Derek later told me in a message that I looked like a man possessed. I was determined to conquer the range that day, and I did. I broke through and made my way to Madrid a day later, and what a feeling it was.

I was my hero as I cycled into the stunning-looking city. My original plan was to cycle right through the centre and out the other side. That plan changed pretty quickly as I cycled into the most beautiful and excit-ing park I had ever seen. I had visited some beautiful parks all over the world, including Kings Park in Western Australia and Gardens by the Bay in Singapore. But Retiro Park in the centre of Madrid was something very different. It had a boating lake, restaurants and bars, statues, stunning gardens and buildings, and even an area that was home to feral cats.

I stopped at a statue near the centre of the park and phoned Sue to tell her that I was in the most beautiful park, but that something was missing. I told her how nice it would be if she came out for a few days. Later that day, her flight was booked, and I had booked into a hotel in a great location just a short walk from the park. It wasn't easy to find a hotel close to the park that had a safe space for the bike. Sue arrived the next day, and we had a wonderful ten days together.

One day in the park, I spotted a small plastic bag next to a rubbish bin, and it looked just like a little bag of weed. I bent down to take a closer look, and sure enough, it was. We bought some papers, tobacco and a lighter, and spent the rest of the day, and a couple of other days, stretched out in the park on the grass with the grass. It was a little trip back to our youth, and a bit of a giggle.

After ten wonderful days with my wife in Madrid, I felt rejuvenated, and after taking Sue to the airport, I spent another night at the hotel so that I could put things in order and get an early start the following morning. My target was Valencia on the coast of the Mediterranean Sea, and I was so excited about it. I spent time looking at maps showing the terrain between Madrid and Valencia. I noticed another extensive range of hills and the Hoces del Cabriel Natural Reserve, and there were gorges and what looked like lots of wildlife in the area. The reserve was about three or four days away or even more, and I was in no doubt that plenty of other exciting things would happen before then.

CHAPTER 4

You have no limits

After leaving Madrid, I took it easy as I worked my chunky legs back into pushing such a sizeable two-wheeled lump. I rode just 20 miles to a campsite. The weather forecast for the week ahead was hot, sunny and dry, and everything looked perfect.

Sue had brought me more shirts and shorts, so I'd swapped them for the older ones in my bags which she took back with her along with a few other things I didn't think I'd need. After giving my bags another proper sorting out back in Madrid, I was able to dedicate one pannier bag solely for food, water and cooking equipment.

I had also jumped on some weight scales at a chemist near the hotel and found I had lost 28 pounds. I knew I'd lost a lot of upper body muscle because I could feel it and see it melt away, though my legs had stayed quite big and strong. I'd have been happy if the weight loss had been all fat, but having hypothyroidism made losing fat quite difficult for me.

My thyroid gland wasn't able to produce enough thyroid hormone, which I needed to regulate my metabolism effectively.

Specialists had prescribed Levothyroxine medication for life, which is a synthetic form of the hormone and designed only to help, and most symptoms remained. As a result, I was susceptible to weight gain, muscle aches, fatigue, feeling cold, sweating, sluggishness, tiredness, low moods and even depression. Without regular medication, I ran the risk of a condition known as myxedema coma, which can be fatal. Some days I would get to about lunchtime and either run out of steam or my muscles would feel like they didn't exist. When symptoms caused me to struggle to the point that I couldn't push myself through, I tried to find a place to stay or camp and finish my ride early in the day. I found what worked best was to put extra effort into covering as much distance as I could from an early start in the morning, when my body and mind were ready to take on the world. I was usually on the road well before 8 a.m., but I would try to aim for 7 a.m. or as soon as it started to get light. Thankfully, I have a can-do attitude that helped me fight through the symptoms.

I arrived at the campsite I had targeted while in Madrid, and I felt great. It also felt great to be back on the bike after such a long rest and returning to my usual routine of setting up the tent and washing clothes. Strangely, it also felt good to be back in my sleeping bag. I had grown attached to my little instant home in a rack-pack.

I had a great sleep, and I started the day by following some dusty old roads that had rubbish piled high along the verges. While dodging broken glass and other waste, I spotted in the distance what looked like a small, makeshift village of tin huts and shacks. At first, it looked abandoned, but as I got closer, I noticed washing on lines but no inhabitants, so I took a few photos with my phone and cycled on. I had a feeling the tiny village was home to people who worked on massive landfill and rubbish sites in the area. A little farther on, a car driver thought it would be funny to come over to my side of the road and drive through a muddy puddle to soak me, which he did. I stopped and waved obscenities at him and shouted a few choice words, hoping he would stop so I could let him feel how I was feeling, but he carried on.

Later that afternoon I found another grubby campsite, and after settling in as best I could, I made lots of calls home. My target for the following day was a town called Tarancón, where I hoped to find some cheap digs.

Early the next morning while I stood at the top of a hill having a drink and checking my phone, a guy on a motorbike passed the other way. I watched as he turned around and came back to ask if I needed assistance. I told him I was only having a short rest, but I was thrilled he wanted to help. Throughout the day, wagons were giving me extra space, and people were waving and honking their horns to acknowledge me as a cyclist. The day before, I was head-to-toe in the vilest-smelling muddy water. It was a scorching day, and traversing the undulating landscape was hard going but enjoyable.

As I rode through Tarancón, I thought I saw what looked like a garden centre with sheds for sale, but then my eyes focused on a sign that read Hostal Gran Avenida. A hostal was usually a cheaper form of hotel, and often more expensive than a hostel, from what I'd experienced. I called in and found that although the structures resembled large sheds, they were quite modern and comfortable. They had fantastic clean shower rooms with towels and soap, and the living/bedrooms had air-con. Other features included Wi-Fi, TVs, fridges, tables and chairs, and comfortable beds. There was space for my bike and plenty of shops nearby. I looked to see if the hostal was online, and I was shocked to find the prices were what I had paid for a nice little hotel room back in the UK. I thought I'd give them a knock and see if they had any special rates for a weary-looking bicycle tourist who was miles from home. After a little haggling and getting the receptionist to laugh, we did a deal for under half the online price.

The next day, feeling refreshed and raring to go, I cycled less than 20 miles and came across what looked like a great wild camping spot, with a single lonely little cloud above it. I pushed the bike in and stood for a moment. Flies circled my head like starving vultures, and the heat was off the scale. I wondered what the hell I was doing. I still had loads of energy and couldn't just sit there for the rest of the afternoon twiddling my thumbs and talking to myself, however interesting I was.

Being concerned about not finding another wild camping spot was no reason to finish my day so early, so I was back on the road. Just a few miles farther on, I found myself outside the Restaurante Segobriga and Hotel, and it looked ideal. I was in no rush, so I looked online for more details and saw there was an offer price of about £20 for a double room, so I headed to the reception desk to enquire further. The receptionist said the room available had a bath. That was all I needed to hear. I hadn't sat in bathtub in so long. There was also a bar and a great looking restaurant in the hotel. Lots of people were coming and going. The staff told me there were a lot of similar hotels near the A-3.

The A-3 was a major Spanish highway that ran between Madrid and Valencia, and I saw on the map there was a rat-run alongside it. Rat-runs, as I called them, were usually small tarmac or gravel roads that ran flush with highways or motorways. Farm vehicles and other forms of highway-prohibited transport used them too. Quite often they were the first roads before new, bigger and better ones, so when looking at a map for the day, I would zoom in to major highways to see if there were rat-runs alongside. The next morning was hard but enjoyable, and I enjoyed it more because I felt I would be able to keep alongside the A-3 until late in the day, then relax in another cheap roadside hotel and restaurant for the night. At about lunchtime, I called into a restaurant next to a petrol station in Cervera del Llano, where I planned on having a nice hearty lunch to keep me going. Inside I couldn't find a menu, and I needed one because the staff spoke very little English. I received only a blank stare from one staff member while acting out my best cheeseburger impression, with sound! I walked out and into the petrol station next door and bought three large bottles of water and a packet of cheese-flavoured corn snacks, which wasn't the hearty lunch I had in mind.

While packing the water and corn snacks into my panniers, I got chatting with two guys who were working there as one of them spoke excellent English. I told them about my adventure, and they loved what I was doing and insisted I wore a high-visibility vest. I told them I had one already, but they insisted on giving me one of theirs, which was much appreciated as it was a lot less bulky than mine. I told the two guys that I hadn't seen another bicycle tourist in Spain, and they told me I was the first bicycle tourist they had seen all year, and given it was the end of summer, it seemed strange. I said to the guys that it was because it was too damn hilly and there were too many flies in those parts, and they laughed. One of them told me, "You have no limits," and then pointed at me saying, "No limits, no limits." They said they watched National Geographic and shows about people like me. I was flattered, and "You have no limits" stayed with me. I liked that a lot.

After a giggle for a few minutes, I bid the guys farewell and cycled on until I arrived at Bar Restaurante La Sima. It was £20 for another excellent room, and although I'd only covered 30 miles that day, I was happy. I settled in and hung my washed clothes on the balcony, before going down to the restaurant for a beer and some lamb chops and chips. £20 plus beers and food might sound a lot of money, which it was when compared with the nights I spent wild camping, but I felt refreshed because I slept and ate so well, and I would be ready to take on the world the next morning. Not that I planned on cycling any farther than the next roadside hotel restaurant.

Staying in digs from time to time made me think of the bicycle tourists who loved to do what was known as credit card touring. The first credit card bicycle tourists I met were back in France, and I thought it was a great idea for short tours and groups. Share rooms to keep costs down, pack a few essentials and a change of clothes onto a lightweight touring bicycle, and book hotels and guesthouses in advance of cycling a set route. It wasn't something I had an interest in, but I understood why others enjoy it.

I left the hotel early in the morning to look for a cash machine in the nearby town of Honrubia. I cycled up and down the town's roads trying to locate a cash machine that was working, and I stopped to see where the next one was on the map. In my handlebar mirror, I could see a small white car parked a short distance back, and I could see a couple of men inside it looking my way. I'd spotted the car a few streets before and thought the guys looked a bit suspicious as they slowly passed me in the opposite direction. I started to feel they may have been thinking about robbing me, but were wondering how to go about it, or waiting for me to get out of town before doing it. Well, I wasn't waiting for an attack, so I got off the bike, took my helmet off and started walking towards them. I wasn't going to wait for two idiots to make a cock-up of robbing me. I might have got hurt that way. I must have looked a bit too big and angry because they drove off.

Strangely, I felt a little disappointed when they drove off. I'd had a hearty breakfast and was just in the mood to take on a couple of cowardly villains. But, all that said, I could have been entirely wrong, and they may have only been interested in what I was doing, and I mistakenly took them for crooks. Regardless, I played it safe.

I gave up on the cash machine idea and continued to what I felt was the best stretch of road of the whole tour to that point. The tarmac was smooth, and the scenery stunning, and I had managed to get away from the A-3's rat-run, cycling for two days on the N-III to Requena.

I wasn't able to locate another hotel before Requena. I had a great night of wild camping in an olive grove, and passing through the Hoces del Cabriel Natural Reserve was incredible. It reminded me of photos I'd seen of the Rocky Mountains in the USA, but on a much smaller scale. It was hard going in parts, but a box of Mars Bars got me through, and I was soon in Requena, where I booked into the Hotel-Motel Sol II.

While checking into the hotel, I was asked by the manager if I was on my own. I told him I was, and then he asked me again. A while later, he came by and asked if everything was okay. He was looking over my shoulder into the room, and it seemed a little weird. The only thing I could think of was that other bicycle tourists or travellers had booked in as one person, but then sneaked others in later. The room was much cheaper for sole occupancy than it was two or more people sharing.

After settling in I went to the restaurant and asked for a menu, and the same manager seated me in a rather posh part of the restaurant. There were white table cloths and wine glasses, while the other part of the restaurant looked more like a roadside café. I told him I only wanted sandwiches or something wholesome and straightforward. He insisted I sit in the posh part and handed me a menu with some fantastic choices at £8 for three courses, and there was a massive bowl of bread to go at too. After the meal, I met a few people on the café side who were on a driving holiday, and we had a good laugh for a few minutes and spoke of our adventures. I even got a big hug from one of them because she loved what I was doing and was a little concerned for my safety on the roads and while being alone.

From Requena, I had less than 50 miles to cycle to reach Valencia, but I was back on the rat-runs next to the A-3 and they were in such bad condition in some parts that I often had to push the bike. One section had a small hill so steep that it looked like a wall from a distance, and I was about to take a photo of it when I saw a head poking over the top. It was a man staring right at me, who then moved backwards out of sight. Curious, I hurriedly pushed the bike to the top, and while catching my breath I could see some movement in the bushes, so I approached with a little caution. Suddenly, and with a rustle of some bushes, a short, elderly gent popped out, and I nearly jumped out of my skin. He looked at me and pointed to the ground a few yards away, where there was some netting stretched out under an almond tree, and it had lots of almond husks on it. Other than a few ohs and ahs, neither of us said a word. We both guessed that neither of us spoke the other's language. He offered me a handful of almonds he had shelled earlier, and they were delicious. We stood together for a few minutes eating before I nodded and tried to say "gracias" as best I could. He nodded and smiled, and I continued on my way. That was a real gem of a moment for me and made my day.

A little farther on from the lovely gent with the almonds, I was stopped by two police officers on motorbikes and asked where I was going. I told them I was heading to Valencia, and they asked where I had started. When I said the UK, they looked at each other and had a little conversation in Spanish, before looking me up and down like most people did. They then held out their hands to shake mine, before riding off.

Continuing, I found myself in a vast orange orchard. It was all I could see for miles, and the oranges looked large and ready for picking. I couldn't bring myself to pinch any, as I didn't think it would have been right, but it was so tempting. I got behind a tractor that was towing a large trailer filled with oranges, but the track was narrow, and there was only enough room for the tractor, which was moving at a snail's pace. I had no option but to pedal slowly behind it in the dust it was kicking up. The driver couldn't see in his mirrors due to the trailer being so broad, so I had no way of letting him know I was there. After a while, the track widened slightly and I had my chance to get around it, and the driver looked shocked as we waved at each other as I passed.

Despite my effort to reach Valencia before dark, I ran out of time. I ended up in a hostel just five miles from the city. I was okay with that because it meant I could spend time enjoying the city the following day before heading up the coast towards Barcelona. The hostel though was a mess. I came across it by chance and booked in without giving the room a viewing first, and that was because they said at the reception that I could take the bike inside. I almost always view rooms first if I haven't booked online and paid in advance. I found that by asking to see a place before paying, I stood a chance of getting a better room than the room the staff had in mind for me. I had in the past even seen receptionists change keys at the desk when I'd asked to see a room.

I instantly felt itchy as I looked around the room and headed for the bathroom. I opened the bathroom door, and a cockroach, the size of a surfboard, fell from behind the door and nearly gave me a heart attack as it ran out of the bathroom and straight under the bed. The size of a surfboard may have been a slight exaggeration. There was also a gap under the door that a small horse could have galloped underneath.

After giving up on trying to find the cockroach, I went out for something to eat and picked up a can of bug spray. I emptied the lot into the room when I got back. I then sat outside for 20 minutes while it went to work, and I could have sworn I heard screams from inside. I then used a bathroom towel to sweep up the half-dozen smaller roaches and other bugs before using it to block the gap under the door. I slept in my sleeping bag on the bed that night.

I made it to Valencia and what a feeling it was. As I cycled through the city, an English guy came cycling alongside and asked if I wanted to join him for a coffee, so I did. Later, as I enjoyed some lunch in a park in the city, a Belgian family came over for a chat, followed by an English family.

I was glad I had time to enjoy the park, and I had a lovely time chilling, chatting, and eating great food.

I then cycled over to the sandy Malvarrosa Beach, which had a long restaurant-lined promenade. I couldn't hang around for too long due to spending so long in the city and park, so I continued up the coast to look for a campsite. After a couple of hours, I came to a site that looked great. It was coming to the end of the holiday season, so I didn't expect there to be many campsites open, and that one wasn't. I knew that as winter approached, I would have to rely on the type of sites that were open all year for permanent residents. Those types of sites were few and far between and weren't usually as well-maintained as those open seasonally for holidaymakers.

I stood outside the gates of the campsite looking for hotels on the map. A couple on bicycles approached and told me that the site next door was open and that they were staying there themselves. It was a relief. Once booked in with the tent erected, they invited me over for a coffee and a chat.

As I made my way steadily along the coast, the landscape became quite industrial. Factories and large featureless buildings spoiled the coastline. Castellón de la Plana was 45 miles from Valencia and quite pretty, and I found a campsite just north of there that provided a power connection and fast internet access. There was also a hose I could use to wash the bike. Before cleaning the bike, I carried out a little maintenance. Ensuring there were no loose nuts and bolts anywhere was something I had to do quite often due to all the bumpy tracks and poor road conditions. I found the pannier rack fixings worked quite loose over time, and I would often get to the nuts just in time. I kept meaning to buy a tube of thread adhesive. After giving the bike a proper sorting out, I made my way to the beach to watch a beautiful sunset.

My camping neighbour was working in the town, and his wife and children lived in San Sebastian. He told me there was a seaside town farther along the coast called Peniscola I had to see, so I set out early with the hope of reaching the town. Later in the day, I ended up on a track that weaved through a national park close to the sea, and it slowed my progress considerably. My desire to hug the coast resulted in me riding a path that was no more than two feet wide, surrounded by chest-deep grasses. It wasn't until I was free of the narrow track that I realised my £100 cycling sunglasses were gone. They were in a case attached to the handlebars with Velcro straps and the straps had rattled free somewhere, so I made my way back along the track but couldn't find them. I was so disappointed in myself, as they were such a great pair of glasses.

Due to poor riding conditions and having to search for the glasses, I failed to make it to Peniscola. I did, however, find a campsite in the Serra d'Irta Natural Park. Mountainbike riders regularly passed me on the bumpy gravel road through the park, and it was hard going, but well worth the effort because Camping Ribamar was quite extraordinary. It was expensive at about £20, but the high price was because all the available pitches were for campervans. After setting up the tent, I used a passkey I was given by reception to open a gate to a path. It led to miles of Mediterranean marine reserve, and I had myself a lovely swim in the cold water.

After a few miles of butt-busting rocks and gravel the next morning, I got a glimpse of Peniscola in the distance and it looked incredible. When I got close, the town appeared to be built on a rocky island, tethered to the mainland by a small strip of land packed with bars and shops. I didn't venture into the main town area, as I needed to find a supermarket and an ATM, and I wanted to keep moving. I preferred to make my sandwiches rather than buy them. I liked to make sure there was something substantial in them, so I bought ham, cheese, and fresh salad from a supermarket, and shoved the lot inside a large baguette. I then sat on a bench near the beach and ate the lot.

With a full belly, I headed up the coast for 30 miles to the Ebro Delta, and it was a comfortable ride due to cycling along many beachfront paths and promenades. A lot was going on, and there were crowds of people around.

Arriving in the Ebro Delta, I was shocked to find myself cycling through mile after mile of rice paddies. I was aware of the popular paella rice dish, but I had no idea that rice was grown in Spain until that day. There were so many birds of all different kinds in the fields too. Herons and flamingos, and many I had never seen before, were all feeding in the shallow waters. Behind, in the distance, was the range of hills I had cycled through to reach Valencia a few days earlier, and it was a spectacular setting. I loved coming across surprises like those rice paddies, which was why I rarely looked too far ahead on the map. It had been a long day, and as fascinating as the Ebro Delta rice paddies were I needed to find a campsite, and I spotted what looked like an excellent site on the map. I cycled five miles to reach it against a strong headwind, but found it shut, along with the campsite after that. I started to wonder if I was going to find a place to stay, as I was in the middle of a swamp of rice paddies; the same swamp rice paddies I'd thought were beautiful just an hour earlier.

I felt my only chance of finding a campsite or some digs was if I made it to a decent-sized town on the coast so, with the wind against me, I headed to L'Ampolla. My chunky little legs had been going around like the clappers for most of the day. I eventually found a campsite just before sunset, where I had a quick shower. I then spent the rest of the evening in the bar, and I was flat out as soon as my head hit the pillow.

I crawled out of my tent on all fours in the morning, and a clear sky and slight headwind greeted me. I was just a couple of days away from Barcelona. After another pleasant stay at a lovely campsite, I arrived in Tarragona. There were demonstrations and roadblocks at several junctions throughout the city that I had to navigate my way through. I'd heard a few days earlier that people of Catalonia were demanding the right for independence from the rest of Spain, or at least the right to vote either way. The demonstrations seemed peaceful enough, and I only encountered one large group of protesters standing toe to toe with police at a junction across a bridge.

I was soon in a town named Sitges, where I found myself on a relatively narrow and winding road. The coastline became hilly, but due to heavy traffic and a concrete barrier, I was concerned that someone would become impatient and try to overtake. I didn't fancy the idea of getting squashed against the barrier. Thankfully, there were a few small parking areas along the road that I could pull into to catch my breath and let traffic past.

Shortly after Platja De Gossos Sitges, which was a small bay area cut into the hillside, I pulled into a parking area and a truck followed me in. Two guys climbed out of it and came over to me for a chat. They asked where I had cycled from, and then looked me up and down when I told them. One Spanish guy asked if I was fit enough for it, the cheeky bastardo. I told him, "I got this far didn't I?" I told them that I found hills to be hard work due to all the weight. We chatted for a little while and had a bit of a laugh. I then continued to Barcelona, and what a feeling it was to get there. Every major town or city I arrived at made me feel like I had achieved something spectacular, but I had to return to the UK.

CHAPTER 5

Captured the unwanted attention of a bull

A few weeks before leaving the UK, I had several blood tests and an examination at a hospital close to home. The result was that my blood was dangerously thick. The haematologist thought the testosterone gel I was using was to blame. He understood why I needed it, but suggested I should reduce the daily dosage by half, or risk a heart attack or stroke. He suggested I cancelled the adventure, and he made it crystal clear I would be risking my life if I left before getting my blood normalised. But there was no way I was pausing my adventure, so I agreed to reduce the levels of testosterone by half.

Another part of our agreement was that I would return for more tests a couple of months later. I had calculated I would be in Spain or southern France at that point, and only a short and cheap flight away. I'd considered having tests done abroad, but I needed to have the all-clear from my specialist in the UK for my medical records to keep up with insurances.

I knew I would be returning home once I made it to Barcelona, and I had booked my return flight a week earlier online. A few days later, my wife called to say that Monarch Airlines was going bust and had cancelled all their flights. I went back online and booked a flight with another airline the same day before they sold out. I knew that as soon as everyone realised the airline was going bust, there would be a mad rush to buy flights on other airlines, and seat prices would rocket. Many people would have left it in the hands of the airline or the UK government to get them home. There was no way I would ever put my full trust in the UK government or an airline that was on its way out. Thankfully, I managed a return flight for less than £100 before the panic set in.

I then had to find a place to secure the bike and gear until I returned, so I did a little internet search and located a handful of self-storage options. I knew I'd find somewhere to store my things, and managed to book a unit just big enough and cheap enough at Bluespace on the north side of the city. Before storing everything, I spent a few hours at a launderette, washing and drying the clothing I was leaving behind. I then folded it nice and neatly and stuffed it in the panniers, ready for my return.

Back in the UK, the haematologist gave me the all-clear. He said my blood had normalised, and I was good to go. I was glad that there was something healthy about me. Being home for a few days gave me time to stuff my face with all sorts of familiar foods like stews, roast dinners, fish and chips and full English breakfasts. I also did some gear shopping to prepare for the oncoming winter in Europe. I bought an expensive and very light folding chair because I was tired of sitting on the floor, some thermal socks and gloves, a woollen hat, and a stainless-steel pan with a lid. It was great being home and it was comfortable, but I wasn't ready to stop. At the very least, I wanted to complete my cycle across Europe.

Before returning to Barcelona, Impact Graphix and Signs in Warrington, Cheshire created an excellent weatherproof and sturdy sign for the back of my bike, which was much better than my old one. There was no charge, which was kind of them. I wasn't sure at first about having any signage hanging off the rack-pack, as I thought it was a bit showy and I have always been quite a shy person, but it turned out to be a great idea. It helped spread the word about JUMP and people came up to me, interested in what I was doing. It also seemed to make things a little safer for me while on the road and made the bike a little more unsavoury for would-be thieves. It made me more visible from a distance, and drivers would slow down to try to read it. Because it was in English, it attracted English-speaking people who wanted to chat. Some would copy my social media details then follow my adventure. I also had a QR code for people to scan to locate my website.

Before I knew it, I was back in Barcelona and collecting the bike and gear and I was excited. I'd booked into a hotel for the night and thought it would be criminal of me to leave Spain without trying a paella dish, especially after riding through the rice paddies farther south. So, I ordered a chicken and chorizo paella in a restaurant where they put me behind the door, out of the way. I often felt poorly treated or looked down on by restaurant and shop staff in quite a few places and couldn't understand why. It was such a different feeling than in France, where it seemed everyone I met, including restaurant workers, were friendly and helpful. I had also met some lovely people in Spain, but mostly in the more rural areas and small villages and towns. I also met some nice holidaymakers and expats. I was so determined to try paella that I sat at the table and ordered, but when it arrived, it looked like a bomb had hit it. I thought I had set my expectations far too high; either that or the staff hadn't been too bothered about the lone, middle-aged guy behind the door. The waiter then lobbed a bowl of bone-dry bread on the table, and I just presumed it was how they served it, but usually without the attitude. Then I noticed that some couples and groups having paella were given bowls of sliced bread with olive oil drizzled over. I didn't feel like creating a scene, so I ate part of what had been lobbed at me and left the restaurant without giving a tip or a thank you.

On my first day back on the road, the bike felt like a tank as I cycled out of Barcelona. I'd brought back a few items, but no more than 20 pounds in extra weight. I was also feeling a little sick, so after just a few miles, I decided to take it easy for a few days to get back into it. I may have had a little jetlag or even food poisoning from the paella I'd had the night before, so on my first day back, I cycled just 20 miles to a campsite. I planned 30 miles for the following day and 40 miles the day after that to get back on track. The site was just £7 a night, and it had a pool, bar, free bus to town, and was right near the beach. After a good night's rest, I was raring to go.

My next destination was Lloret de Mar, and the first three campsites I came across weren't open. Thankfully, the fourth one was, though I couldn't see anyone around at first. I eventually located a staff member who lived on the grounds and who gave me a little plot out of sight. I was the only guest, and the place had just one toilet that wouldn't flush and only one cold shower working. There was no shop or reception area, and I was charged £8 for the pleasure of staying there. It was only the day before that I had paid £7 at a site with everything open and with excellent facilities. Getting a decent campsite was hit and miss out of season, but I wasn't in any position to complain much. I let the staff member deal with the toilet once I'd left on my way to Palamós.

Before arriving on the coast, I had a vision in my mind of endless, flat, sandy beaches peppered with cheap, tacky bars, but for the most part, it was so different from that. At a campsite in Palamós, which I thought was beautiful, I spent the evening on the beach with a few snacks, soaking in the views and listening to the waves crashing.

From Palamós, I travelled some great cycle paths that reminded me of those I had ridden in France. The wind made for tough going though, and it was a struggle to keep a good pace, but the views were so lovely and the weather so sunny that I didn't care all that much.

For the next two nights, I stayed at campsites. At the first, I had a great night of drinking beer and eating pizza, while stretched out on a wooden deck chair. Shortly after arriving at the other, I started to wash my clothes in the shower with me. I then realised, in the scrubbing frenzy, I'd also scrubbed the clothes I'd wore to the shower block and had nothing dry to wear. I only had a small, dry, microfibre cloth, so I put a bundle of wet clothes over my butt, and my wash bag and towel over my private parts, and made a mad dash to the tent. I was embarrassed, as it was busy around the shower block, and people looked on in horror. Luckily, I had other clothes to wear to the bar.

As I headed for the French border the next morning, I got to thinking that nothing unusual or of real interest had happened since I'd cycled out of Barcelona. It was as a blessing in one way, because anything of interest with me often meant something not so good, which sometimes even hurt. Then, late in the afternoon as I fought hard against a strong headwind, I realised I had no chance of making it to the border before dark so I located a campsite on the map. As I cycled along the N-11 towards Camping L'Albera Capmany, I pulled into a petrol station to pick up some water and a few snacks. As I pulled out and back on the road, I couldn't believe my eyes. Young adult women, wearing skimpy bikini bottoms and short T-shirts, and the highest of high heels, were stood at the side of the road touting for business. I could only presume they were prostitutes, as I hadn't passed a bar or club along my route. I had never seen anything like it. I felt myself blushing as I cycled past each one until I turned onto another road towards the campsite. Well, that added interest to the day, I thought, and it didn't hurt a bit.

At the campsite, a lovely elderly English couple who were travelling in their campervan greeted me. They asked if I needed anything picking up from the supermarket in town, which was nice. I thanked them but said I was okay, and they handed me a cold can of beer. I then had myself a refreshing cold shower in the campsite's lovely clean shower block. Walking back to the tent, I spotted a family-sized bar of chocolate on my camping chair. They were such a lovely couple to have done that, and the following morning they gave me some more food to see me on my way and told me about a road through the hills that would take me over the border into France.

Thank heavens for that bar of chocolate and all the goodies the couple gave me. I needed every ounce of energy as I headed through the small town of Espolla and along a road that led to the border. At first, it seemed like a gentle, continuous climb. However, it soon became apparent I'd be climbing for miles through the lush green hills of the Paratge Natural l'Albera, which was a nature reserve of stunning beauty.

While enjoying the scenery, I spotted a big black mass at the side of the road in the bushes, no more than half a mile ahead. As I got closer it became clear it was a huge bull, just like the bulls I'd seen in bullfighting images, and it didn't look happy. A road cyclist came down the hill and passed the beast at speed. It nearly jumped out of its skin and looked a bit shaken and angry. I thought it was going to take its anger out on me. I was going uphill and didn't have the option but to pass the bull at anything but a snail's pace, so I got off the bike and put it between myself and the beast. I crept past it, trying hard not to look at it or spook it into doing something silly as it stared right at me. I looked at my clothing and bike to make sure no bull triggers were showing. There was a cliff to my right beyond a barrier, and the banks had lots of shrubs and bushes, but I got myself ready to jump into the bushes if the bull decided to charge. Thankfully, it just made a few grunts, and I carried on up the hill.

I eventually made it to the top, and I was exhausted. My thighs felt like they were burning, but it was going to be downhill to the seaside town of

Banyuls-sur-Mer in southern France. I had my disc brakes on for much of the first part of the descent as it was extremely steep, and every so often I would release the brakes to give them a little chance to cool. I was fully aware of the amount of weight I was putting on the front wheel and forks, so I tried to steer and brake as smoothly as I could. Once on the gentler slopes, I cruised along and enjoyed every mile of it.

Once on the coast, I cycled on some lumpy and hectic roads for quite a while until I found Camping Les Criques de Porteils. It looked great, so I booked myself in for two nights to rest. I had an excellent pitch overlooking the sea, and there was a bar on-site. I set up the gear-shed and threw my bags inside out of the way. I then had plenty of room in the main tent area. I inflated both of my air mattresses, starting with the cheap £20 mattress I set out with, which was okay, but I'd had to patch it up a couple of times. When I flew back to the UK from Barcelona, I treated myself to an expensive £100 Therm-a-Rest mattress to help keep me warm at night. I set up my new lightweight OEX table and Helinox chair, and the pitch was complete. I cut small holes in four tennis balls and put one on each foot of the chair to stop it sinking in the ground under my weight. I also had a power cable and power supply going straight into the gear-shed.

I was able to do some video and image editing on the second rest day, and spend a little time chatting with loved ones and responding to comments on social media. The day before, when I'd first arrived at the campsite, a couple of people stood watching me as I rode to my pitch, and we said hello to each other. They came over to me after I'd booked in and introduced themselves as Emile and Trees. They were a lovely couple from the Netherlands and were impressed with my effort.

I thought about how I'd been cycling for 72 actual days, not counting the short trip back to the UK. It was a big first-time solo bicycle touring adventure in itself.

As I continued up the coast, I came across a big black horse standing in the road looking at me, bowing its head and moving its legs as though it was about to charge. It reminded me of the bull that had spooked me a couple of days back. I didn't know what to do. I was worried it might get hit by a vehicle. A guy pulled up in his car and managed to get it into a field. He appeared to be calling it by a name that I couldn't interpret.

The wind was furious that day so on finding a campsite that also rented static caravans, which they called lodges, I booked myself into one out of the wind. The strong cold winds that regularly passed through the area were known as Mistrals, and the coastline was popular with kite surfers. The wind was so strong that day that the tent might have been ripped to shreds if I'd tried to erect it. After making myself comfortable in the lodge, I went over to a bar on the site and met a couple from Belgium having a drink, and they bought me one. We sat together talking about all sorts of things, including my adventure. I needed to eat, so I bought them both a drink and said goodnight.

I could feel the temperature starting to get colder, so I hoped to reach Greece and maybe even Turkey as quickly as I could, but I had a long way to go before Greece.

A couple of days later at a campsite close to the coast, I awoke to the sight of a large bulge in the side of my rear tyre and I had no idea what could have caused it. I could only think that the soft rubber on the folding tyre walls wasn't tough enough for the kind of punishment I was putting them through. It was also Sunday, so there were no bike shops open, and I still had a fair distance to cover that day. I decided to cycle with it, but it was painful, like cycling over a rock with every revolution. I carried a spare tyre, but I didn't want to use it in case other damage had been caused. I decided I'd only use it to replace the bulging tyre if it blew. I booked into a hotel later in the day and had a good rest nursing my aching, bleeding butt.

It was Monday morning as I cycled to Bump Cycles in La Grande-Motte, where the guys fitted a new tyre. It was no Marathon Supreme, but it was wide enough and looked like it would keep me going for a while.

Later that morning, I rode through the beautiful Camargue Natural Regional Park. It was stunning, and flat, yet rugged. I captured some lovely images of Camargue wild horses. The horses are one of the world's oldest breeds and indigenous to the Camargue region. I spent most of the day following canals, and I came across a couple of bicycle tourists with their two children who were having lunch at a picnic table. I also passed a female bicycle tourist with long blonde plaits trailing from her bicycle helmet. She was sat on a bench eating an apple, so I stopped to say hi, but she looked at me and looked away and continued eating her apple like it was the only food she'd eaten in weeks.

Sometimes, other bicycle tourists would cycle straight past me without so much as a nod. I encountered quite a few like that who would do their best not to make eye contact. I had never been like that; I'm the kind of person who will say hi to everyone, and I'd always try to make eye contact. It sometimes bothered me when I encountered those I thought of as miseries. It may have just been a cultural thing; maybe they were from a miserable culture.

The Camargue Natural Regional Park was impressive, but the grinding from the hub had returned. It seemed worse than ever. It felt like the back wheel was ready to collapse.

The next day after a night in a guesthouse, several calls and emails exchanged between me, KOGA, Rohloff and my dealer, and I had to make a tough decision. I couldn't send the back wheel to Rohloff because they'd simply apply more grease and send it back, they said. I felt the problem was more serious than an operational noise. I had no idea how KOGA would receive me if I took the bike to them in Heerenveen, Holland, given the treatment I had received at the shop in La Rochelle, and there were no offers of assistance in getting the bike back or fixed in southern France. I knew the issue would get resolved to my satisfaction if I returned the bike to Cyclesense in the UK, and I was sure it would take more than a blob of expensive grease to put right. I just wanted it fixed once and for all.

The relatively short distance back to the UK made my decision easy. I was closer to the UK than when I was on the Mediterranean coast of Spain. I needed to get the bike back to the dealership in one piece and couldn't risk it being lost or stolen, so taking it back by car was the safest way. If it became damaged on a flight or lost, I would have had no chance of getting a full refund if I needed it, and as I'd spent more than £4,000 on it I wanted it sorted. I hired a people carrier car in Marseille so that I could get the bike in the back, and I started driving the roughly 660 miles across France to Calais. It wasn't fun, or cheap, but I tried my best to put it down to being just another part of my incredible adventure. I stopped a few times in rest-stops and services to take short naps when I felt myself drifting off.

At one stop late at night I was messing around with the car's interior light, trying to get it to stay on while talking to Sue on the phone. I noticed something moving in the bushes. It was like a scene from a zombie movie, as a sorry-looking middle-aged man stumbled out and stood in front of the car, staring at me through the window. A nearby street light made him quite easy to see, and I watched as he made his way slowly to my door. I talked Sue through what he was doing, and as he stood there looking in, I told her I'd phone her back after seeing what the guy wanted.

He then started pressing on my door so I opened it, pushing him slowly backwards. I asked him what he wanted, but it was clear he couldn't understand English because he didn't reply. Instead, he started using gestures to indicate what he wanted to do to me sexually. I couldn't believe it at first, and I was in a sort of shock and didn't know how to react, but it soon sank in, and I belted out a string of choice words and sent him on his way. He was so lucky I didn't react more harshly. I then phoned Sue back and told her what he wanted. I couldn't understand why the guy would approach me like that, and I wondered if switching the lights on and off in the car was misunderstood as a come-and-get-it signal. I was careful with the interior lights after that. I was even concerned about putting the headlights on at the next stop, in case they attacked en masse with their pants around their ankles.

After a few naps through the night and a lot of road tolls that were quite expensive, I arrived in Calais. I dropped the car off and caught the ferry to Dover in the UK, before picking up another car and driving up to Liverpool. I had driven roughly 1,000 miles in all. A much shorter route than I'd cycled. I was home and shattered and felt I could have slept for a week, but I had arranged to drop the bike off at Cyclesense in my car the following morning. It seemed strange that after a couple of months of cycling across all sorts of terrain through England, France and Spain, it took me less than two days to drive home.

I planned to get things sorted as quickly as I could and get back to southern France to continue from where I'd left off. I needed to get back on the horse and not give up or wallow in self-pity, but I did feel a little sorry for myself. I couldn't bear the thought my journey could be over if I couldn't get the bike fixed or a full refund to buy another one. It wasn't like I could have changed the rear wheel to run derailleur gears either, because the frame could only accommodate a hub according to my dealership.

I dropped the bike off at Cyclesense in Tadcaster, and they later carried out the thorough investigation I knew they would. It turned out there had been a lot of wear on the carrier. My dealer was in contact with KOGA, Rohloff, and Gates, and he kept me updated through telephone conversations and emails as they got together to work on a solution. We eventually agreed the repairs would be at no cost to me, of course, and Rohloff management and I also had a telephone conversation to discuss a few options. We agreed I would go with a chain rather than the carbon belt. The hub, which was in perfect condition, was serviced and remained. It was only the exterior components that had led to my return.

The sprockets were changed to accommodate a heavy-duty chain, and I was provided with plenty of spares and tools.

A great little extra freebie was a Hebie Chainglider, which was a chain guard in two halves that clipped together over the whole of the chain and front and rear sprockets. It was a clever bit of kit that didn't attach to anything. It used the chain movement to appear to hover, and there was no feeling of drag. They also thought the glider was ideal for helping to keep my leg and clothes grease-free. The carbon belt was good for that until the guys in La Rochelle put grease on it. There would also be less dirt and grime on the chain and sprockets, prolonging the life of those parts. I had a new bottom bracket fitted, and two new Schwalbe 50mm tyres and tubes.

I'd had the craziest time on my adventure; it was everything I had expected, and a whole lot more. I knew that if I could make it through Europe, I'd be eyeing India. From experience, getting a visa for India wasn't a simple affair. It wasn't that difficult, either, but I felt that trying to get one while cycling through Europe might have been hard work, so I sent off an application with ID and had a 12-month visa in less than a week. I thought that even if it took me half the year or more to reach India, I would still have plenty of time to enjoy it. I wasn't sure I would get there, but for the sake of an hour completing an application, it was worth it.

Aside from spending a little time with my wife and children and catching up with friends, I contacted Stanforth Bikes. We talked about their great looking handcrafted touring bicycles built in the UK. I asked them if I was stuck somewhere on the other side of the world and needed a sturdy new bike, how long it would take them to get one out to me. They told me they would get one out quickly, for a great price and to my specifications. They assured me they would support me no matter where I was in the world. I wanted to know, just in case I had more problems, and needed to parcel my bike home while still wanting to continue my adventure. Although I felt reasonably confident that the bike I had would do the job, especially after all the work that everyone had put into it.

Two thousand miles, a face down to the floor, four hire cars, and two ferries after leaving southern France with a broken bike, I was back with a smile from ear to ear and ready to continue my journey around the coast to Monaco and beyond. I felt confident the chain drive setup would take a beating from a super heavyweight bicycle tourist with shit-kicking legs. Rohloff let me know they would follow my adventure on social media and would be a phone call or email away if I needed their support.

CHAPTER 6

Lost and found

Toulon was a lovely town with a great feel. I cycled leisurely through and came across a mobile pizzeria restaurant serving one of the best pizzas I'd had in a long time. I thought the idea of a mobile pizzeria was fantastic, and I got to wondering how it would work back in the not-so-sunny north-west of England where I lived. I imagined it outside a nightclub, serving great food, playing great music, and me throwing drunken louts through the plastic windows of a rain shelter.

Back in the '90s, a late friend of mine, Ian Scott, and I owned a large catering trailer that we affectionately named Big Dicks Hangout. We would set it up on weekends outside a nightclub in Warrington in Cheshire, and we were doing splendidly, until a night that ended in tears. Thankfully, though, not our tears. A mob of about a dozen idiots tried to turn the catering trailer over while we were still inside. We stepped out, and they moved back and started throwing rubbish from a dustbin at the trailer. When the dustbin was empty, they yanked it from the ground and threw that, and it bounced off the side of the trailer. We asked them to stop and told them we had families to feed and were trying to earn a living, but our pleas fell on deaf ears.

Ian held one of our carving knives, and I had a wooden police baton. Bouncers from the club came over and asked if we needed any help. They had been watching what was going on. We told them we'd be okay, as the louts had started to get into taxis. A short while later, only the two ringleaders remained. They insisted their mates got into taxis before them, and they continued to curse at us while waiting for their taxi. They looked quite proud of themselves.

We felt two against two were better odds, so needless to say we dealt with them. Just enough to get our feelings across. We knew they'd be back another night to cause more trouble with more louts, so we decided to call it a day. Earning a crust that way was just too much trouble. And so, maybe, a mobile pizzeria wouldn't be such a great idea back home, at least not for me.

I liked Toulon, and I met loads of smiling people, but I had to head up the coast and into some hills to Camping Manjastre. At the start of a hill climb, I stopped to check the map and lost my footing, falling upside-down into a ditch. Thankfully, it was a dry ditch with lots of deep grass to break my fall. I had the bike on top of me but managed to claw my way out quite quickly, before dragging the bike out and checking it over for damage. I then made sure there was nothing left in the ditch.

At the campsite I was given a pitch under a shelter, so I was able to wash and hang up my clothes. I had to set the tent up on a cold concrete patio, but I hoped my two mattresses would keep me warm. I also had my goose down sleeping bag, thermal leggings and top, and another top, thermal socks, as well as tracksuit bottoms, woolly hat and gloves. But after about an hour, I was sweating like a pig and had to strip off.

From the minute I left the campsite the following morning, it was uphill through a series of steep switchbacks with no hard shoulder, just a ditch, and I wasn't a fan of those. It was a busy road, too, and seemed a significant route for quarry wagons. The day before, my map apps were instructing me to take to the coast, which would have added another 15 miles, but like a fool I chose the shorter route. That said, despite the tough going, the scenery was spectacular, and once over the top, I had a beautiful valley to cycle.

Later in the day, I was back on the coast with a great view of Saint-Tropez across a bay. The campsite I had in mind that had stated it was open, wasn't, and I'd run out of energy. I checked the internet for hotels or guesthouses nearby and found myself a cheap hotel. All I wanted to do was chill, so I dropped all the gear off and went to the beach to watch the sunset over Saint-Tropez.

I had a great sleep at the hotel, and my next stop was Saint-Raphaël, and another comfortable night in digs, followed by a day of strong head-winds and heavy rain. I didn't mind putting up with rain from time to time, as long as I could end the day nice and dry in either a bed or tucked up in my sleeping bag. I had a few more days with not much happening other than rain and wind, and I was desperate for the sun to come out and something exciting to happen. Eventually the sun did come out, and I was smiling again. I always felt so much better when it was warm and sunny.

The south of France had a lot of beautiful coastline with a lot of wealth on show, but Cannes felt filthy rich. Bentleys and supercars lined the roads, and it looked like a lifestyle for the truly rich and famous. I parked my bike next to a few large luxury yachts and wondered what it must have been like to live like that. I made such good progress that day in the warm sunshine that I skipped the campsite I had planned for and made my way to one I had planned for the following night.

The next morning, I was excited to get going. I continued along the coast, out of France and into Monaco, then Italy. It was strange to think I had cycled just 45 miles and been in three different countries on the same day.

The rain was back for my first full day of cycling in Italy. After riding into Imperia, I stopped to take a look at the map and noticed I'd cycled right past the campsite I'd targeted. It was raining and dull, but I was fixated on the stunning scenery and forgot to look out for it. I then doubled back to the south side of Imperia to the campsite and, as my luck would have it, the sign on the gate read closed. I got chatting to a couple of people near the campsite gate, and they gave me bottles of cold water and directions to another campsite back on the north side of Imperia. So it was back through Imperia in the pouring rain, and I eventually made it to the campsite. It looked closed, but I made my way to an old house with building materials piled up and broken cars outside. I knocked on the door. An upstairs window opened, and a girl shouted down that someone would be with me in a minute. The rain was so heavy that I couldn't have got any wetter, and there was nowhere to take shelter. Eventually, I was greeted and given a pitch.

I carried a large plastic tarp which I was able to tie above the tent to a fence and a couple of trees. It helped keep my tent and bike nice and dry underneath, and I could sit out under an overhang. There seemed to be dozens of campsite cats, and a few came over and sat with me to keep me company, not that I was a big lover of cats. It was nice to have a little company, though I didn't want to encourage them in case they decided to stick their claws into the tent. With dinner and coffee safely in my extended belly, I showered and watched a movie on my laptop while the rain thundered down outside. I fell asleep in no time at all and slept like a log.

In the morning, one of the cats was still there, and I felt a bit mean packing up in the rain and taking its shelter. The weather forecast was rain and more rain, so I called ahead to a campsite a further 15 miles up the coast to make sure they were open. I decided to have a short day due to the shitty weather. I couldn't just stay in the same campsite for days in the rain; it would have driven me scatty, with cats for company or not.

With the rain and wind doing their best to beat me down, I just kept my head low and plodded on until I came to a hill that kept me busy for quite some time. I couldn't go any faster than slow against the wind, and the road looked like a raging river. The road was so narrow that drivers couldn't help but splash me as they passed in their vehicles. I tried cycling on the footpath, but vehicles were then able to go through the deep puddles in the gullies and drench me even more.

Getting to the top of the hill was a relief. Standing under my umbrella while catching my breath, I looked over the barrier. I nearly cried as I stared down at a flat coastal bicycle path. I had looked on maps that morning to see if I could see any sneaky cycle paths, but I couldn't.

I arrived at the campsite to find the only spot available was a lump of tarmac under an inch of water. Surely my day couldn't get any worse, I thought, and I almost wished I had stayed where I was the night before. I obviously couldn't set my tent up on a submerged campervan pitch, especially not for the asking price of £17. I was wet and shivering and my chest was aching with the cold, so I booked into a hotel less than a mile away for £22, and it included a great breakfast. I was able to dry all my gear and get changed into some warm clothes and have a tasty evening meal in the hotel before diving into white sheets on a sprung mattress. If I had been travelling with another person, I would have been able to share the cost of hotels, but £22 wasn't so bad, considering the benefits over the duck pond offered at the campsite. Thank goodness the weather picked up the next morning. If it hadn't, I would have stayed nice and snug in the hotel.

Making my way along the coast the next day, I passed through Andora and Borgio Verezzi, and I ended the day by going out for pizza and cutting my hair with my electric shears. My wife, being a barber with her own business, had given me a few pointers for managing my hair while away, and I became pretty good at it. Some young cyclists I passed in France looked like wild animals. I liked to keep tidy if I could, and it gave me something extra to do with being on my own.

I continued on some amazing cliff roads with spectacular views, and I met some friendly people and even had my picture taken a few times. Later in the afternoon, I was stopped by police in Varazze. They said I would have to choose a different route because the main road around the coastline was temporarily shut. Cyclists in the Milan-San Remo bicycle race were on their way through, so I quickly looked for some digs, and I got myself a real bargain, right on the main drag where the riders were due to pass. I had already done enough distance that day in the rain and only had 23 miles to cycle to Genoa. After dumping my gear in the guesthouse,

I rushed out and stood on the side of the road to watch the race, and I couldn't believe how fast the cyclists were. It was incredible, and later I heard the winner had completed the more than 180 miles in around seven hours. That distance would have taken me about four days.

It was then back to my room to get a shower and sit down for an evening meal in the guesthouse. It was a simple setting, and I sat with people who appeared to be residents; some of them were very old and needed assistance to eat. The meal was terrific; a lasagna that was a vivid green and seemingly made with a lot of cheese. I had never had it before, and it was so filling.

After a great night's sleep, I set out in the rain for Genoa with a plan to arrive early in the morning. I had booked a hotel for two nights in Genoa because I'd noticed a ticking noise from near the hub a while back, and it was different from the time I'd had to return to the UK. I thought the sound was similar to when I had changed gear on my old hybrid bike with a derailleur set-up, a sort of chain rattle. I contacted Rohloff while I was in Grimaud in southern France and told them about it, and true to their word to support me, they got straight to it. They arranged for me to call into Bici Shop Genova when I was passing through Genoa, and they instructed the shop to change the splined carrier to the threaded carrier. I was given the threaded carrier as one of my spare carriers back in the UK and kept it in my repair bag. I was also given a threaded carrier fitting tool.

I had timed my arrival in Genoa for the shop opening early in the morning, and the owner and his family greeted me with big smiles and friendly faces. I was back on the road in no time, with a new chain fitted too, and Rohloff kindly dealt with the bill. It was great to feel I had Rohloff and Cyclesense onboard. I'd booked to stay for two nights because I didn't know if I'd have to leave the bike at the shop, and I also needed a couple of days of rest.

I managed to do a little sightseeing in Genoa, and I had the most delicious pizza at Ristorante Pizzeria Vicolo in the Sestri Ponente district. Cycling around the city was treacherous though, as cars would pull out like I didn't exist, and it wasn't like a 5XL, wearing a bright yellow vest was inconspicuous. So many drivers in Genoa seemed to be some of the worst I had experienced, and I had a few near misses. One ancient lady driver turned the corner of a street I was passing, forcing me to roll with her as my bags rested on the side of her car while I shouted for her to stop. I made a racket as I hit against the car, but there was nothing from her. It was astonishing, and I was pretty sure that if I had gone under the wheels, she still wouldn't have noticed. I managed to come to a quick and safe stop with people looking on like it was my fault, and the lady continued on her merry way, seemingly oblivious.

I might have been a bit harsh on Genoa, and what I perceived as a hard exterior could well have been a beautiful and vibrant city if I had given it a chance. There was quite a funny moment on my second day when I stopped at a harbour-front café for lunch. The small building had large glass panels, and I tried to enter by pulling open a glass door that just wasn't budging. I pulled with quite a lot of force, and as I was heavy-handed and an expert at breaking things, I wasn't doing the building a lot of good. People inside were standing up, yelling and waving their arms as I yanked at the door. Just seconds from me levelling the building, a member of staff slid it open. He looked like he was about to cry as he pointed to a sign on the glass. I shrugged my shoulders and told him I didn't speak Italian. He then looked to the sliding door and pointed to a directional arrow. I was a bit red-faced, but it must have been scary for those inside to see such a big, angry-looking person trying to rip the building apart. Two days of rest in Genoa was enough - and two days of rest was always enough, no matter where I was when on my own.

My ultra-vague plan for the next two weeks was to continue along the coast to Naples, passing through Pisa and Rome on the way. I had a couple of tough hilly days after leaving Genoa and going to Sarzana. Thankfully, it then got a little flatter for a while.

A ferocious, icy crosswind spoiled the warm, sunny weather. As I cycled on a major road that had tree roots tearing up the tarmac and no shoulder to ride on safely, I took a battering from the wind as it tried its best to blow me off the road. As I fought one way, the draught from passing wagons would pull me the other, and a couple of times I had to get off the bike and wait for gaps in the traffic so I could edge my way along. It was quite frightening, but I still managed to cover a fair distance that day.

I had seen the Leaning Tower of Pisa in hundreds of photographs and videos. Still, it was nice to pop by and take a snap of my own. There were thousands of tourists, and trying to push my bike through the crowds was hard going. There were market stalls and touts and sellers of all kinds, and sadly there were a lot of armed soldiers and other security measures in place. I thought it was a real shame that people couldn't visit such attractions without feeling 100 per cent confident they would make it home in one piece.

The tower was great to see, but 15 minutes of staring at it and I was back on the road again, heading towards Rome. I expected to be there within just a couple of days. I needed to take it easy and keep safe in the horrendous road conditions.

As I cycled south, a lot of the coastline of Tuscany was beautiful, especially from San Vincenzo. Marina di Grosseto was an area I particularly enjoyed in the warmer weather I experienced. I had been averaging around 45 miles a day and thought, if I could keep that pace, I would be doing just fine. Cycling 45 miles a day was roughly twice what I was often doing when I first set out. I could only imagine how lugging my bulk 70 miles a day or more might feel.

I had completed more than 100 days of cycling, not including my returns home for blood tests and bike repairs, and I was feeling like a star. My daughters were often putting posts on their social media, telling their friends how proud they were of me. I had about 20,000 social media followers, though not all of them had any interest in what I was doing. Many were following to get followed back, as was the social media norm, but I felt a fair few might have had a real interest. It was always good to respond to comments and see post likes. It was like having a little company pushing me on, and it was good to share my experiences each day.

After a couple of great days, I arrived on the outskirts of Rome. I booked into a hotel, dumped my gear, cycled to a train station and headed into the city to take in some of the attractions. The Colosseum was something I was excited to see, and it was impressive. I cycled for a couple of hours in the city and took plenty of snaps and video, and had a fun afternoon. It was then back to the hotel for a nice meal and to sleep in a soft double bed.

The next morning, I felt it was time to give all my clothes another good scrub, so I located a launderette. I was okay with washing clothes at the end of each day in the shower or bath, but nothing could beat a good washing machine clean. I put all the darks in with the whites, and everything was considerably lighter out of the spin-dryer. There must have been a lot of sand and dirt in the clothes. I was surprised to find that my whites were still the same as they were before they went in almost white. Despite a couple of hours at the laundrette and having something to eat, I made good progress along the coast and spent the night in a guesthouse.

It was time to do a little planning. I worked out that it would take me a couple of long days to reach Pompeii, so I booked a room in a guesthouse in advance for two nights. Pompeii was a place I especially wanted to see, more so than the Leaning Tower of Pisa or the Colosseum. Ten minutes of planning complete I slept like a baby, and I was soon back on the road on a bright and sunny morning.

I hadn't been on the road long when I came across the most beautiful graffiti underneath a bridge. I put the bike on its stands and took some photos using my phone and placed it on the rack-pack. I then took out my Sony camera and went back across the road to capture some more images.

All done, I cycled up a very steep hill to a junction and stopped to take a look at the maps, and I nearly died when I realised I hadn't picked up my phone off the rack-pack and it was gone. It was such a busy street.

It had taken me quite some time to reach the top of the hill, and as I looked back down towards the bridge, I could see a woman with a child just standing and looking up the hill at me. I raised my arm straight with my hand stretched out flat, in a sort of, "Hello, do you have my iPhone X?" kind of way. She raised her hand, and I could see she had something in it, so I guessed it was my phone and within seconds I was with her.

She had picked it up off the ground and was looking around when she saw me looking down the hill at her. I thanked her and gave her my cycling business card with my name and details on it. I went to hand her €20, but she said no. I asked if she would give it to her daughter as a thank you for doing such a good thing, and maybe she could buy some ice-cream. She nodded, and the little girl's eyes lit up as she looked to her mum. I had just had my £1,000 phone returned, and there were credit cards and a load of cash in the phone wallet, so I was thrilled, and back up the hill and on my merry way.

Later that day, the scenery changed drastically - it was as though I had crossed a bridge, and everything turned black and white and truly grim.

There was nothing pretty; well not to me, on a stretch between Castel Volturno and Lago Patria. Broken glass and rubbish lined the route, piles of refuse bags with dogs and people picking through it all everywhere. Prostitutes seemed to be every hundred yards or less on both sides of the road for quite a distance. It wasn't as though it was after dark either, so I could only imagine what it would have been like once the sun went down. I had never seen anything like it. Young girls younger than my daughters, or so they appeared, reduced to or forced into prostitution, plastered in make-up, wearing crazy high heels, and hailing cars that went by.

I had, earlier in the day, booked a room in the Hotel Mirage in Giugliano in Campania, and it was a relief to get off the streets and into the hotel. The hotel was just south of Lago Patria, and it was great. After settling in and getting a nice hot shower, I popped over to a supermarket across the street and bought some supplies and thought I'd cook myself a meal on my stove on the balcony.

I'd just started cooking some pasta when I realised my phone was gone. I took the room apart trying to find it, but with no joy. I then thought I must have placed it on the counter in the supermarket, or dropped it somewhere outside, so I got back to the supermarket as fast as I could. I imagined someone being away with it for sure, but as soon as I walked into the shop, an assistant told me that I had left my phone on the counter.

It was such a relief, but I was getting a little tired of being an idiot with my phone, especially as it was such an essential bit of kit. I had a cheaper phone in my bag as a spare just in case, but I preferred the new one. I had been lucky in some ways with the new phone, but I wasn't quite so fortunate with it the following day.

CHAPTER 7

Everything I'd imagined

I was glad to be out of the area and heading down the coast again. Halfway through the morning, I stopped at a small café to grab a coffee and a bite to eat. It still looked a bit rough where I was, so I took my phone out of a plastic phone sleeve attached to the handlebars, and I went to put it in the pocket of the hi-viz vest I'd chosen to wear that day.

It wasn't a pocket at all, it was an air vent, and everything seemed to go in slow motion as I watched the phone make its way to the floor, face down, and it made a loud smack as it touched down. I picked it up and turned it over. I could see cracks starting to appear towards the centre of the screen. The screen protector didn't help because the phone had hit the floor at a slight angle and the corner hit first. I was devastated.

I usually listened to map directions through a single earphone while the phone itself was tucked safely away in the handlebar bag, but quite often it would fall out of my ear, or I'd receive delayed instructions to turn at a junction that I'd passed many yards back. So I decided to try a plastic phone sleeve I had in a pannier. That way, I could at least view the screen.

The display amazingly still worked, but I knew just a little moisture getting in would have killed it. I looked online at new screen prices, but because the phone was Apple's latest top-of-the-range model, I was looking at about £400 to get it fixed. I wondered if it could hold out until I arrived in India, where I might have been able to get new glass fitted cheaply. I got way ahead of myself, as I wasn't even sure at that point if I'd make it out of Italy, let alone another country.

I eventually arrived in Naples, and the traffic was as bad as it had been in Genoa. Cars were pulling out or seemingly trying to squeeze me against parked cars, and people were just walking out into the road like they didn't have a care in the world.

It felt great to get through Naples and make it to Pompeii in one piece. The hotel was pretty crappy and not at all like the images online, but the historic sites were just around the corner. I couldn't get internet access in my room, so I went down to see the manager, who told me there was no Wi-Fi in that room, so I asked for another. She said there were no more rooms available, and I could use the Wi-Fi in a seating area near the reception. I brought my laptop down and logged on to see if there were any more rooms available, and there were. I told her that according to information on the internet, there were rooms available. She said I had the last one and that the information needed updating. I didn't believe her, but I was in no position to argue because I couldn't find another room in another hotel so close to the ruins. The view from my room was onto a wasteland, with rubbish and graffiti on all the surrounding walls. It turned out I didn't need to go any farther than my hotel room to see ruins. I also had a family next door that sounded like they had a dozen unruly children and several farm animals. But I settled in with my headphones on, and it didn't take me long to fall asleep.

It was a wet start to my first day of rest in Pompeii. But it soon picked up and turned out to be a beautiful day to visit the historical and archaeological sites. I was impressed with the ruins, and it was the floors in the buildings and the roads that impressed me most - probably due to my life in the building industry and decades of groundwork. Some of the tiled floors were beautiful, but I just had to see the body shapes of the people that had perished. There was a dog, a small child, and quite a few adults. The amphitheatre where gladiators fought was impressive too, and I was surprised at just how sprawling the sites were. My stay in Pompeii was excellent, and I enjoyed the few days of rest.

I had a brainwave during my stay in Pompeii, and because my brain-waves were often more like brain freezes, I had to go over it a few times in my mind and sleep on it. I decided that, because I only had a few days left in Italy, I would cycle from Foggia down to Brindisi. Both cities were in the Apulia region, but a few days of cycling apart. I wanted to experience some coastline along the Adriatic Sea, instead of just cycling east overland to reach Brindisi. I much preferred cycling coastlines to farmland. My plan was good, but it meant I had to make up the days somehow. The ferry to Greece wouldn't wait around, so I decided to catch a train from Salerno going north to Foggia, then cycle for a few days down the coast to Brindisi.

I cycled 20 miles from Pompeii to the port in Salerno and set up my fishing tackle and did a bit of spinning to see if I could catch my supper. If I'd had to rely on fishing to feed myself, I'd have starved to death.

The city of Salerno was not too shabby, but rubbish littered the beaches and plastic bottles were knee-deep in places. I hadn't seen a soul clearing litter or debris from beaches in the parts of Italy I had cycled. I often saw broken glass sticking up from the sand, which I promptly removed when I had the chance. I couldn't bear the thought of a child running merrily towards the sea and standing on it.

My arrival in Salerno meant my journey of more than 1,300 miles around some of the Mediterranean's incredible coastline from Valencia was complete.

It took me a while to work out how to get a ticket from the ticket machines with my bike to Potenza, which was my first stop, as there were no trains to Foggia. I was scheduled to arrive in Potenza late in the day and thought I would have to stay there overnight.

Getting a fully loaded bike on a train was a real treat. It wasn't just the weight, but the shape of the bike and gear, and the two flights of steep stairs to reach the platform. Just as I got near the top of the stairs, an idiot tried to squeeze past me. I couldn't believe it. I was sweating like a pig, and I had the bike close to one side of the stairs so that people could pass. The idiot insisted on trying to squeeze into the few inches between me and the handrail. I said to him out loud, "Are you f-ing serious?" He froze on the spot and looked at me in shock. I then used the language barrier-breaking words of, "f-off!" which of course he did.

I was not usually that colourful with my language towards other people. I was just so annoyed, in pain, exhausted, and not in the mood for people like that. I didn't want to take the bags off because it would have meant leaving them or the bike at the bottom of the stairs, and it didn't look too secure that day at the station, with it being so busy. Not being able to run due to spine damage meant I wouldn't have been able to do much about someone making off with my gear.

The train didn't arrive in Potenza until 6 p.m., and it was getting dark. After rolling my bike downstairs to get off the platform, I looked to the top of the opposite staircase. I saw a lit sign stating the train for Foggia was leaving in eight minutes – from the same platform I had been on - so I lugged the bike back up the stairs. After the experience I had in Salerno trying to get tickets, I knew I didn't have enough time to get to the machine and back. So I thought I'd get on the train and just see what happened.

Luckily, I got speaking to a lovely and kind 21-year-old Chinese student named Nuoqi, from Beijing, who was living in Foggia and was on her way there. She was fluent in Italian and English, and she was able to chat with the train guard who was checking tickets, and I was good to go. Nuoqi asked where I was staying in Foggia, but I hadn't had a chance to book anything because I didn't think trains were going there that night. She recommended a cheap-but-nice hotel not far from the station, so I booked a room there. She then walked me to the hotel, because it was in the direction she was walking anyway. On reaching the hotel, we said our goodbyes and wished each other well. I did ask her if she wanted me to walk her home with it being dark, but she said she felt safe and was fine. It was great to have company for so long; I'd missed it.

Rested and refreshed the next morning, I cycled 50 miles from Foggia inland to Barletta on the coast. Sadly, it was just like everywhere else; knee-deep in rubbish, which was a real shame. The landscape would have been lovely otherwise. I could only imagine how many rats there were in Italy. How people didn't end up with deadly illnesses, I had no idea, or maybe they did and I just never heard about it.

I hoped the coast was going to be much cleaner and more beautiful, as I still had a few days to ride to reach Brindisi. It was mostly farmland to the coast, and I was surprised by the number of African migrants in the area. There was a large community on the coastline before Naples, but it was much busier on that coast, and there was more chance of them finding work nearer Naples, I thought. The farmlands seemed empty, with the odd, small, run-down town along my route. I saw migrants in fields where the crops had all but gone, digging for what appeared to be any remaining root vegetables.

It was a strange and quite sad sight and not one I had expected, but I had seen many unusual things on my adventure, and I knew I was going to see many more.

I had a great sleep and some good food at the Hotel Dei Cavalieri in Barletta. I couldn't even be bothered to look for year-round campsites because hotels were less expensive out of season. I tried my best not to leave blood on the bedding from my butt and inner thigh sores and abrasions. I would wear underwear, shorts, and sometimes tracksuit bottoms; anything to stop me scratching the wounds as I slept if they itched. I had to wear extra clothes in my sleeping bag, too, because it would have been hard to remove blood stains from a down-filled sleeping bag. I had bled in the bag, but thankfully not a lot.

The following day got off to a great start, with the hotel manager cracking open a couple of expensive bottles of ice-cold water to fill my water bottles with. I then left the hotel car park with a smile from ear to ear, not only because I'd had a good night and the staff were great, but because there was a strong wind on my back and the sun was shining. I looked forward to riding as close to the coast as I could for my last 110 miles in Italy.

After a few hours of cycling it was clear it was much cleaner on the Adriatic side, and I saw my first person collecting rubbish from the beach. The water also looked super inviting, but the strong wind had a bit of a chill to it, so I skipped the dip.

Just north of Bari was the quiet but pretty fishing town of Santo Spirito-Catino-San Pio. It was there that I watched dozens of small boats coming in with fresh prawns and other sea creatures. It was fascinating to watch them pour their catches onto market stall tables. I spent a short time in the town, but I needed to keep moving.

I did feel I was rushing at times, but because I was on my own, I never felt like hanging around. Not only that, but the pull of not knowing what was around the next corner or what could happen next drove me to keep moving. I often thought about what I could have missed along the way, but what I did see and the experience was wonder enough. I felt that if I ever went on another bicycle tour it would be much shorter, and I would make even more of an effort to take things in around me. But that was a big if, and in the meantime, I just felt I wanted to keep going while I was physically and mentally able.

I thought to myself that my back could give in at any point during my journey, leaving me unable to do anything at all for many days or weeks. It happened quite often, and one time I was stuck on all fours on the living room floor at home unable to move. The pain was excruciating, and I was still in the same position when the ambulance arrived. I was in the hospital for weeks in traction with weights strapped to my legs to pull my spine. My back going like that was always on my mind, especially at night before I went to sleep. It was while I slept that it would usually go.

As wacky as it seemed even to me at the time, I thought about packing a small drone. I would have been able to attach a note to it if I was stuck wild camping in my tent in the bushes out of sight. But I wanted to stay as positive as I could, so I scrapped the drone idea and the GPS tracker and the carrier pigeons, as I'd have only eaten the pigeons anyway! My spine issues were another reason why I liked to stay in campsites or other populated places as much as I could. I was just pleased it had held out for as long as it had. The cycling appeared to be doing the trick.

My next stop along the beautiful coastline was Monopoli, where I managed to secure a room in a guesthouse in the middle of town. I had to cycle nearly 40 miles to get there before 1 p.m. to get the room's access key. If I didn't make it in time, I would have to wait until after dark to collect it.

I met a family along the coast who insisted I visit the town of Polignano a Mare, which was on the way to Monopoli. It was an incredible sight, as many of the town's buildings looked to hang precariously on the coastline's cliffs. There were also caves underneath the buildings that had been carved out by the sea, and it was truly incredible. The coast had turned a little rough and poorly maintained, which was no doubt due to the lack of people in the area, but the small fishing villages made up for it. I arrived in Monopoli as planned, thanks to the strong wind at my back. The digs were stunning, with a curved stone ceiling and ultra-modern furnishings, and it was in what they called the Old Town. After showering and getting into some clean clothes, I put a pile of clothes in the washing machine then hung them out to dry. I then wandered around the town, taking in its beauty and having a nice pasta meal. I finished off the day in a tiny bar, sipping down a few beers.

Fully rested from the most beautiful of soft-sprung beds, I cycled out of town and continued towards Brindisi. Later in the day, I passed a female bicycle tourist who was going the other way, and we both said hi. There was a fair distance between us when I remembered the obstacle course I'd had to traverse a few miles before we said hi, where tarmac had turned to a path covered in rubbish. Then, when the path ended, I'd had to climb over a deep bed of seaweed and crap that had built up in a small bay, which must have once been where a river ran to the sea or still ran to the sea at times.

After pushing and fumbling over the seaweed for what must have been 15 minutes, I came to a six-foot concrete wall. I then had to lift the bike and bags over the wall, which was no fun at all. I felt so sorry I had forgotten about that obstacle course and failed to let her know. But then I felt, because she was a solo bicycle tourist with dusty and tatty gear that looked like she had been on the road for some time, she would have found her way through no problem. It was even more likely the obstacle course was something only I could have stumbled into, and she would have found a great cycle path instead.

I booked into a guesthouse just 20 miles from Brindisi and planned to catch the ferry to Patras in Greece the following day. My host kindly printed out my ferry boarding pass, and I was all set. I was so excited at the thought of getting out of Italy and seeing what Greece had to offer. I had met some fantastic Italians on my cycle through Italy. I'd also had some great experiences, and I thought that if I were to cycle Italy again, I would cycle the Adriatic Coast. It was much quieter and digs were cheaper.

I was just about to settle in for the night when I received a phone call from Direct Ferries. There had been a mistake, and my ferry to Patras didn't exist, and another Patras ferry would be days away. My heart nearly hit the floor. I didn't want to be hanging around for days, and I let the agent know just how annoyed I was. He told me I had another option. I could still get a ferry the same day as planned, but not to Patras. It would be going to Igoumenitsa, the capital of Thesprotia. Well, it was all Greek to me, so I asked him where it was, and he said it was 200 miles north of Patras. I told him I planned to cycle east in Greece, not south, and if I accepted, it would add at least another four days of cycling south, just to Patras, before I could even start heading east.

I asked if I could sleep on the idea and get back to him. He was okay with that and gave me his direct number and the best time to contact him. He also let me know I would have an outside cabin to myself with a shower room. Before I went to sleep, I looked on Google Earth and saw that the landscape in north-west Greece seemed quite lumpy, but the coastline looked stunning. It didn't look like a part of the country that would be thick with tourists, either. It seemed like a great opportunity that I was fortunate to have the time to take on.

Late the next morning, after breakfast and packing my gear, I contacted the agent. I told him I would accept the ferry to Igoumenitsa. The only issue with my arrival in Greece was that I wouldn't get there until midnight. Luckily, I managed to book a hotel ahead of arrival that had a reception open 24 hours, and that would be fine with the bike, and it was just a few hundred yards from the port.

I arrived at the port in Brindisi, three hours before departure, but as I had a cabin, they let me on straight away. I had a nice shower, watched a movie on my laptop, and had plenty of sleep. I was packed at 10 p.m. and ready to get off the ferry for around midnight, but for some reason, it arrived in Greece at 2 a.m. The dock was unlike any I had seen. It was wide open with no fences or restrictions, and I was able to walk the bike off the ferry and across the road to the hotel. I didn't need much sleep after such a long time in my cabin, so I was up early and enjoying breakfast, which was very different from anything I'd had.

My eyes nearly fell out of their sockets when I saw the buffet breakfast choices on offer. There was a basket full of red-dyed boiled eggs, cereals, toast, fruit juices, and meats, including lamb; everything I was going to need to keep me going all day. A member of the kitchen staff told me they always dyed the eggs around Easter, and it was a tradition. I loved eggs to start the day on because I'd feel full for hours. While in Italy, there were often eggs for breakfast, but rarely adequately cooked. In one case I cracked what looked like a boiled egg, but it was raw, and I made a bit of mess. So at my first hotel in Greece, I carefully cracked open a purple egg in case it was runny. It was good to go, so I shoved six of them down my neck, after peeling them, of course, then a bucket-load of cereals and milk, and nearly half a loaf of bread. I was stuffed and felt like cancelling the day and going back to bed.

As I started cycling away from the hotel, I saw some lads fishing on the dock, so I decided to join them for half an hour. While the lads were ripping fish out of the water like fishers on a tuna boat, I caught nothing. It was a beautiful setting. The water was crystal clear, and the sun was rising nicely like the temperature.

It took me some time to cycle up the hill out of the port, probably due to overeating at breakfast, but the views were spectacular. Farther along I passed a few small closed shops, and then a tiny petrol station. The petrol station was closed, but a toilet block attached to it was open. I dug through a couple of bins for empty water bottles, rinsed them out and filled them from the tap in the toilet block. I left with a gallon of extra water because I didn't know if I was going to find anywhere open. The heat and hills were exhausting.

Later in the day, I located what looked like a great wild camping spot on a hill with a spectacular view out to sea. I got into position and was just about to put my tent up when I started seeing bees around my head. I then spotted a dozen or more beehives close to some bushes and decided to look for another place to camp. I passed a few similar spots that looked great for camping but had lots of human-made beehives.

I cycled on and dropped down from the hills to a beach lined with lots of small guesthouses with lovely well-maintained gardens, although the beach looked like it needed a bit of maintenance. It was April and out of season for international tourists, and so it was a little quiet. It was a great time of year. The roads had hardly any traffic, and I expected hotels and guesthouses would be cheap.

I spotted a small guesthouse on the map, charging just £15. On arrival, I felt I must have been in the wrong place. It looked amazing and was right across the road from the beach. So, just in case, I gave them a ring to ask for directions and was told to turn my head around. Waving to me from the porch was what looked like the whole family who owned the Haus Maria guesthouse. My room was clean and spacious, and it had a sea view balcony. After settling in, having a shower and washing my clothes, I made my way to the reception, where the family had just finished eating dinner. They asked me to sit down and presented me with the tastiest lamb and potato meal and, after dinner, I went over to the beach and took in the views for an hour with a couple of beers. It was the perfect end to a fantastic day. I was so pleased I took the offer of a different port.

Back in my room, I was sat on the bed writing my blog when I felt the bed moving. I looked across to my bike in the corner of the room and could see it shaking. Then the whole room started shaking, and it was the weirdest of feelings. I thought a train might have run nearby, or maybe a big wagon. The following morning, as I cycled along the undulating coast road in the direction of Preveza, I came across a spot that bulldozers had very recently cleared. A local cyclist stopped and told me the area was prone to earth tremors and landslides, and the shaking I had felt was likely the tremor that had caused part of the hillside to fall away and block the road. We had a good chat and I cycled on, hoping I wouldn't vanish under tons of earth.

The day had started interestingly, then about an hour later I saw a small lump in the middle of the road, and as I took a closer look, I could see it was a little tortoise. I couldn't believe it. I had watched bicycle touring videos online and loved how cyclists came across animals like tortoises. It must have been scared and was hiding in its shell, afraid to move from the centre of the road. It looked a little worse for wear too, so I picked it up and put it next to some long grass. It didn't move for some time, then all of a sudden it was gone. I didn't realise tortoises could move so fast.

That tortoise made my day, but the day wasn't over. A short while later, I arrived at a tunnel entrance at Preveza. Cyclists weren't allowed to cycle through the tunnel that went under the mouth of the Ambracian Gulf to Actium. It would have taken me two days to cycle around the gulf, whereas going through the tunnel was only a few minutes by car. I had read that if a cyclist waited at the side of the road where cameras could see them, operators would send a vehicle to pick them up. So although I doubted that rule would apply to me, being me, I thought it would at least be worth a try, so I stood at the side of the road staring at the cameras like a raving loon. Sure enough, a few minutes later, a pickup truck headed towards me. The driver signalled that he would be turning around and coming back for me shortly, so I took my bags off the bike while I waited. He arrived about five minutes later and we threw everything on the back, and I was on the other side of the tunnel in minutes and for no charge. I later arrived in the beautiful town of Vonitsa and found a room at the Hotel Pegasus.

In the morning at the reception area, the elderly lady who had booked me in the night before asked if I was ready for breakfast. I told her I could eat breakfast at any time of the day, which got a little giggle. She sat me down and made up the table, then out came the food. A Greek coffee, which I loved, boiled eggs sliced and covered in olive oil, cubes of cheese, biscuits for my coffee, and then a small plate of lamb and two slices of bread. I bet she had never seen a sandwich like it. Afterwards, she asked if I would like more food but, weirdly I was full.

While letting breakfast settle I looked at the map for the few days ahead, and I had a few hills to climb; nothing mountainous, but big enough. Dogs didn't help much, either. I had been chased down the road by small packs of big Greek Shepherd dogs that had me pedalling like the clappers to make my escape. I later realised the best way to get past the dogs was to get off the bike as soon as I saw them and just walk.

I came across quite a few big dogs as I cycled along the E55 to Amfilochia. A pack of six dogs came at me while I was bursting blood vessels on a steep hill, so I got off the bike and stood behind it. Thankfully, a farmer came along on his motorcycle and moved them away by beating a stick against the floor. A little while later, a pack of smaller dogs were put off by my GoPro, which I held out in front of me on a selfie-stick. They didn't like it for some reason and backed down, and I realised I had a great new weapon for yapping, ankle-biting dogs.

I survived another day, and the view across the gulf from the hills was spectacular. I rode into Amfilochia and settled into the Hotel Oscar, and it was just the right price. It even had a balcony where I could hang my washing. I had 60 miles to go to reach the Rion-Antirion Bridge, located just 10 miles north of Patras, where the original ferry from Brindisi was supposed to have taken me.

I was in no rush to cover the 60 miles because I loved the ride and landscape, the people and the food of north-west Greece. It had been everything I'd imagined, and my favourite place to cycle. But even though I was in no rush, the next day the cycling was so enjoyable that I covered the 60 miles with ease, hills and all. On reaching the bridge I found bicycles were prohibited, but thankfully there was a ferry every few minutes. I could have easily hopped on one, but I decided to spend the night in a hotel near the tiny port and catch a ferry the following morning. I didn't know what to expect on the other side of the Gulf of Corinth, so I started the day early with plenty of energy, just in case.

No sooner had I got off the ferry on the other side of the Gulf, than I got a puncture. To save time, I replaced the old tube with a double-ended inner tube. It wasn't a continuous loop like a regular tube, but straight like a broom handle with two flat, sealed ends. It looked like a grey snake, and the idea was that if I was in a rush, I could cut the old tube out without taking the wheel off, then fit the double-ender. I didn't want to be messing about in heavy rain or on a tight busy road or in another situation where it would have been hard to do a quick and safe repair. I also initially didn't have a clue how easy or hard it would be to take the rear wheel off. I had the hub and carbon drive belt when I started my adventure, and the belt needed to be tensioned correctly. I also thought the tube was a novel idea, and at least worth a try.

Just a mile from my planned campsite, I got a puncture in the double-ender, but I made it to the campsite where I removed the wheel and installed a standard inner tube. I also put on the spare tyre from my bag. On closer inspection of the double-ender, there was a kind of burn or graze with a slight cut in it, and I wondered if it was a fault before purchase that opened up under pressure, or the result of both ends of the tube touching and rubbing while I rode.

After doing the repairs, I dived into the crystal clear sea and washed all my dirty clothes in it. It was funny to see people looking on as I stripped off and washed my clothes with a bar of soap. I could have scrubbed them in the shower block, but I thought the salt in the water would do them good, and there were no kids about so there was no harm, although my clothes were in that much of a state that a few fish might have gone belly-up.

Making my way to Corinth the ride was relatively flat, and I had a lovely lunch at a beachside restaurant. I then headed straight past my planned campsite because it looked like a rubbish dump. I planned to reach the port at Piraeus, and then do a bit of island hopping to Turkey.

I continued along the coastline past Megara and caught the ferry to Salamina. I then cycled a few miles across Salamina to catch a ferry to Perama, from where I had to cycle seven miles to Pireas to catch a ferry to Rhodes. I was exhausted due to all the messing around. It was my fault for wanting to see Salamina; I could have simply cycled right around the coastline to Pireas, but that would have been the smart thing to do. When trying to buy a ticket to Rhodes from Pireas, I was told by a bad-mannered and downright rude assistant that I needed to get to Paros first, then catch the ferry to Rhodes from there. While on my way to Paros, a crew member said to me that the boat was like a bus and had several stops to do, and that I wouldn't arrive in Paros until around midnight. I wasn't happy with arriving so late at night, but I was glad to be heading in the right direction. I managed to book a hotel on Paros for the night and fell asleep in no time at all.

The following morning at the ticket office, I found out I shouldn't have been sold a ticket to Paros, because there were no ferries to Rhodes from there. I should have been sold a ticket to Siros and gone directly to Rhodes from there. That annoyed me, because the night before, the boat had stopped at Siros before Paros. The bad-mannered assistant in Pireas had put me on a bum steer.

While I waited for the boat to Siros, I went for a cycle and met an elderly gent who told me a few stories about Paros and his life. It was always good hearing stories from others instead of me babbling on with my own. The ferry to Siros arrived there at 6 p.m. I then had to wait five hours for the boat to Rhodes.

Eventually, I rolled the bike off the last ferry, and it was a great feeling. A few days before arriving in Rhodes, I'd felt I needed a good rest to recharge my batteries and enjoy some time to heal the sores on my butt and upper inner thighs. It was also soon to be my 55th birthday, so I phoned Sue and asked her to book a flight and meet me, which she did. She was due to arrive in Rhodes two days after me. It was the earliest flight she could get with such short notice. As soon as I arrived, I called her and asked her to start looking online for available hotels on the north side of the island.

She then had me cycling up and down a search area of about 15 miles. I also looked to see what I could find, but I arrived at some hotels which looked nothing like the online descriptions. Pretty much anything was suitable for me, but I wanted Sue to be comfortable. I cycled up and down for a few hours before we settled on the Aegean Breeze Resort in Fanes, an all-inclusive hotel on the coast.

Sue booked it online because I was about ten miles away from it after going back up towards the port to look at another, not-so-good hotel. She had mistakenly booked the hotel from the day she was due to arrive, leaving me with nowhere to stay for two nights. She didn't realise when she booked it that I was in limbo; she was just so excited about getting out to see me.

With our hotel booked, I found an excellent hotel for myself for two days. I had a little self-contained bungalow right next to a pool, and I was able to wheel my bike inside out of the way. When Sue told me the price of her flight I'd paid for, I couldn't believe it. I could have cycled for months on that, but it turned out that the only seat she could get was business class. Yeah right, I thought. I found it quite funny, and she deserved a comfortable flight to Rhodes. It wasn't like my adventure wasn't costing me a fortune, though I was glad her return seat home was in economy.

On the day Sue was due to arrive I cycled ten miles to the hotel, passing the airport along the way. After cycling into the hotel grounds, I was straddling the bike and talking to some of the hotel guests. The hotel manager then came over and asked me to leave. I said to him I might look like a lost soul, but I'd made a booking and gave him my name. He then went to the reception and returned to apologise.

With all the bags on a bike and with me looking like I'd been dragged through a hawthorn hedge backwards, I couldn't have looked like a paying guest at a luxury resort. After settling in, I phoned a car hire company, and within a couple of hours, they dropped off a clean white Audi convertible. I wanted to treat Sue for coping without me for so long and managing everything at home.

For 12 days, we drove all over the island and had a great time, but it was soon time for Sue to return to the UK and for me to continue east into Turkey. While enjoying our time together, my mind ran a hundred miles an hour as it usually did. I wondered whether I wanted to continue and whether I felt happy enough with my achievement that I wanted to go home. But, after some serious soul-searching, I decided I wasn't ready to go back. I wanted to see some more of the world on a bicycle. We said our goodbyes at the airport, and I stayed an extra night at the hotel so that I could do a little bike maintenance and get my gear ready for Turkey.

The following morning, I made my way back along the coast to the port and caught the fast ferry to Fethiye. My new, vague plan was to cycle a couple of hundred miles of Turkey's coastline to Antalya. From Antalya, I would box the bike and fly out to Mumbai, India before monsoon season.

The route I planned to Antalya was simple: I'd stay on the D400, which was a major road that would carry me through hills and towns along the coast, all the way to Antalya. I had read online that it was better to cycle from Antalya than to cycle to it, due to easier climbs the other way. Me being me, nothing was ever going to be easy, but I was cool with that. I didn't sign up for easy, although I'd had it more than comfortable in Rhodes.

Arriving in Turkey, I couldn't believe how beautiful it was. The first thing I needed to do was get a SIM card for my phone. The mobile plan I had in the UK that was good throughout the EU was no good in Turkey. I bought a SIM card with 6GB of data for just £10. I then stumbled on what looked like a nice hotel. I asked for a room and said I needed to take my bike inside the room or some other secure area, but the manager told me I could leave it in a vehicle parking space on the street. I thought the guy was joking, but he wasn't, and he continued to point at the empty parking space with nowhere to lock the bike. I wasn't going to leave the bike on the street, so I cycled up the road and found another hotel that let me take it inside.

Outside the hotel, I was surprised to see trucks spraying mosquito killer into the air. I had never seen anything like that before, but it was a great idea. The room was just £12, including breakfast. There were a handful of other British tourists at breakfast who did nothing but complain that the food options were limited. I told them I thought the food was great for the price. I had eggs, meats, bread, and cereals, as well as coffee, tea and fruit juice.

One of the tourists asked me how much I'd paid for the room. When I told him, he turned the colour of boiled shite. He must have spent a lot more. The breakfast was great but I was feeling a little sick, and it was a rare thing for me to feel sick.

CHAPTER 8

The shits and giggles

It was a long, steady, slight climb for a few miles out of Fethiye, but it was so enjoyable. I had no idea where I was going to sleep at the end of the day and didn't care because I was so excited about just being in Turkey.

After 40 miles of hills and heat, I completely ran out of steam. I had done far too much after chilling in Rhodes, and I was exhausted and still feeling sick. It may have been a bug or a bit of seasickness as a result of a bumpy crossing from Greece, or I may have had heat or sunstroke. I hadn't a clue, but what I did know was that I couldn't continue for much longer. I was shaking and sweating profusely, and my vision was slightly blurred, which wasn't the safest way to cycle.

Some distance ahead, I spot a tortoise that was about to attempt to cross the D400. It was the cutest little critter, and not flat and gnarly like the tortoise I rescued in Greece. I stopped and picked it up and walked it back to the long grass and pointed it in the opposite direction away from the traffic. I doubted it would have managed to cross four lanes of traffic without getting flattened.

I then came across a great little spot at a road junction that I thought would make an ideal place to spend the night. It had a steel canopy covering steel benches, and there was a wooden table in the middle. Behind the seating was a shallow, tiled trough and a lot of taps. I had no idea what the place was. I presumed it was a place to rest and wash before praying or eating. There was also a large electric water cooler, so I was able to fill my bottles with cold, clean drinking water. There was also a small toilet block.

I looked up the road to see what was ahead of me, and I could see a large hill. I was still feeling very ill and my head was pounding, so I decided I would move the table from between the chairs and set the tent up, which was hard work. I had to keep sitting down to rest, and sweat was rolling off me. It took me about an hour to get organised. I still had a little energy left, so I cooked some pasta on my burner, washed just a few items of clothing, and had a good scrub.

Earlier in the day at a petrol station I was welcomed by the friendliest of staff, who gave me a cup of tea and some tomatoes and chilli peppers. At another petrol station, the guys gave me tea and fruit juice. I had never met so many friendly people in such a short distance, and most of the people I passed appeared to be happy and friendly. I had no idea what Turkey would be like before I arrived, although I'd heard varying opinions. The roads were in fantastic condition too, and drivers would give me plenty of space as they passed. It was such a shame that I felt so ill.

I added the tomatoes and chillies to the pasta and then sat back. As it started to get dark, I was surprised and delighted to see the light come on under the roof of the shelter. With thunder and massive bolts of lightning all around, I was so glad I had chosen not to continue, and I was cosy and felt very safe. I slept like a baby.

As I crawled out of the tent the next morning feeling much better, I was greeted by a dozen chickens and a goat. I made coffee on the burner and walked around to stretch my legs, and as I looked across the road, I realised I was at a cemetery. I laughed out loud, and the animals scattered like rats from a sinking ship. I couldn't believe I'd slept there and so soundly. I didn't think I'd upset anyone by camping there, because everyone that passed seemed to nod their heads as a way of saying hello. I was back on the road at 6.30 a.m. to beat the heat, and I arrived in Kalkan before lunch.

I still didn't feel 100 per cent so I decided to stay the night in Kalkan and not push my luck, and I found some great digs for £12, including breakfast. I enjoyed my first couple of days in Turkey, despite the illness, and I was in no rush to cover crazy miles each day, so I cycled just 15 miles the next day to Kas. I booked into a beautiful campsite next to some clear water where people were snorkelling, and I had a small chalet with air-con. I had no interest in sleeping in my tent when other options were so cheap, and I still wasn't feeling great.

While chilling in the chalet, I went to work on a plan for India. I wasn't even out of Turkey, but I thought it would be a good idea to make some sort of plan. I already had my visa for India, so I thought I'd try to get there before the monsoon set in.

Before I knew it, I was cycling through Demre, which was roughly 28 miles from Kas, then Finike, before arriving in Kumluca, which I didn't like, so I kept moving. After checking the map, I knew I wouldn't find a hotel or place to stay before dark, so I wheeled the bike into a clearing in some bushes at the crest of a large hill and set up camp for the night, and I slept like a log. It was very hilly between Kumluca and the coast in the direction I was heading, but the landscape was beautiful.

Later in the day I found an all-inclusive hotel for under £20 a night, so I decided to give it a go. After settling into a dump of a room, I went for dinner in an outdoor restaurant located at the front of the hotel, and the food was horrid. There were bowls of tasteless cabbage, boiled potatoes and a sort of stew which was also devoid of taste, or meat. It was a proper bland-fest and let-down.

I ended up going along the road to find some Turkish food, which I had been loving. Breakfast at the hotel was the same as the lunch and evening meals: dull and tasteless. I had just finished my breakfast of stale bread and a coffee, when I noticed the cook gathering up the leftover bread from tables and plates. He put the lot into a sack, then emptied the sack contents into a basket - the same basket he had taken it out of before each meal. I couldn't believe it. I'm so funny with food that I was nearly sick at the thought of eating bread that could have been on someone else's plate. Every guest other than myself was Russian, and I couldn't understand a word they were saying. It was in Russian, after all, and my Russian was less than rusty. Every one of them ignored me for the time I was there, and even though the hotel was busy, I felt more alone there than I did when wild camping.

The last part of my cycle towards Antalya was through a series of tunnels on the D400, and the road became a tad tighter due to not having any safe shoulders for me to ride. Also, I didn't know what it was about the last three tunnels I rode through, but I was so nervous. I'd cycled through so many around the coastlines of southern France, Monaco, and especially Italy. Although some were a bit tight I still felt quite safe, but those last three in Turkey felt very different, and one seemed a mile long.

Other than that, I had an incredible ride along the D400. I loved the scenery but I loved the kindness of the people even more, and I told myself I'd return one day.

From a hotel in Antalya, I made my way to a bike shop nearby. I wanted to see if they could arrange a cardboard bike box, and even dismantle the bike and pack it securely for me, as I hadn't a clue. Taking it apart was one thing - putting it back together again in India might have been something different. The staff at Bikehouse Antalya agreed to provide the box and pack the bike securely for the flight, and it was much appreciated. I told them I'd help so that I could understand how everything went back together.

I then took a trip out to the airport to arrange my flight, and I should have guessed it was never going to be straightforward. I spoke with staff from several airlines, who told me it would be two flights - one to Istanbul and another from Istanbul to Mumbai. I had no problem with that. The problem was, they could only guarantee my bike would be on the first flight, not the second. They said I'd have to get the bike off the first flight that would land at one airport, then take it to the next airport myself and ask if I could put it on the second flight. Not one airline I spoke with could book the bike through to India. I couldn't see a way around it at first, other than booking one flight to Istanbul and staying in the city while I arranged a second flight to Mumbai.

I really couldn't be arsed with all that, so I decided to fly to Manchester in the UK from Antalya, then fly out to Mumbai from there. That way, the bike would go straight through from Manchester. I would also get to see my wife and children and pick up more tyres, spare tubes and other bits of kit.

After booking my flight to Manchester, I then spent two days enjoying Antalya before boxing the bike. The guys at the bike shop had it packed in no time, and it was much easier than I thought. It was just the front wheel, wheel guard and rack, seat and seat post and pedals that had to come off. The beauty of the Atalanta handlebars was that they were easy to either fold down or come apart in two pieces that I could strap to the side of the frame. I padded the bike with my sleeping bag and items of clothing. After taping it all together in case the box got a hole in it, fastening parts with plastic ties, and letting the air out of the tubes, I was good to go. It was important to let down the tyres. The bike was going to be in the hold, and the pressure might have caused a problem. I also cut small holes in the box, so customs staff could inspect the tyres without having to rip open the box. One of the guys from the bike shop took me to the airport in his pickup truck, and I was soon on my way, once again, back to the UK.

A couple of people I met in Antalya asked me why I wasn't cycling through Iran and Pakistan to get to India. I told them I'd heard Iran was a beautiful place to bicycle tour at one point, but I had no interest in wanting to see it, let alone cycle across it. I felt the same about Pakistan and the other stans surrounding Iran and Pakistan. I had no interest in Russia, China, Bangladesh or Myanmar. I only wanted to cycle in countries I had an interest in visiting. The thought of cycling for weeks or months on my own through countries I had no interest in would have no doubt driven me crazy, or crazier! My journey was never about cycling through as many countries as I could to reach a certain point and then return home. It was about wanting to enjoy each country I chose to ride through. I loved that I could do pretty much what I wanted when I wanted and how I wanted. I felt I would never again in my life get the opportunity to take on such a huge adventure. After all, I was closer to fifty than I was to sixty when I started cycling from Cheshire. By the time I arrived in Turkey, I was closer to sixty. I thought that was quite funny, considering I was under the impression cycling was supposed to make me feel younger.

I had covered thousands of cycling miles, and although I returned to the UK three times, I accepted it as part of the experience. I was lucky to have been able to afford to do it that way. Every day of my adventure was eating into my life savings. I was living one of the most incredible experiences I'd ever had, and I considered it worth the sacrifice. I knew my bicycle touring adventure would be like nothing I had read about, and I was cool with never knowing what was going to happen from one day to the next. I also had no idea how long I would stay in India, or whether I would take off somewhere else in a different direction.

Back in the UK I only had a short time before leaving for Mumbai, so I made the most of it. Sue had a leg of lamb, pea soup, and lots of other foods I liked, lined up. It was great to catch up with my daughters too, as I hadn't seen them since I took the bike back to the UK from southern France, which seemed such a long time ago.

Before I knew it, I was back on a plane. I was so excited. But I was also sad to be leaving again. I had driven a car in India some years earlier, so I had an idea what it would be like to ride a bicycle there. I would need eyes in the back of my head. Getting used to riding on the left again would be strange, I thought, especially after touring for so long on the right since leaving the UK in 2017. I planned to keep close to the coast in India to take advantage of places to stay and, I hoped, meet regular tourists or even bicycle tourists.

My flight to Mumbai involved a changeover in Dubai, and I was about to take my extra legroom seat on the second plane when a flight attendant approached. She told me the chair wasn't in operation, and I could see the seat row had a gaggle of unruly children crawling all over it. The flight attendant asked me to follow her into the next cabin and pointed to an empty seat and asked if I would accept that seat instead. My eyes lit up, and I jumped at the offer. Whether I got the upgrade because of the kids or because there really was a problem with my original seat, I didn't care. A glass of bubbly and an actual hardcover menu for meals gave me a smile from ear to ear, and I sunk into the thickly padded seat. I had never been able to justify paying more for anything above extra legroom in economy class, so I savoured every minute.

I arrived in Mumbai and expected there to be people everywhere, but it was strangely quiet. The temperature was 35°C, with high humidity and very little wind, so within minutes I was sweating.

I managed to get a big enough taxi to take the bike to Basti Backpackers Hostel, which I had booked into for two nights. I couldn't stop myself from laughing for most of the short drive from the airport, as cars weaved in and out, horns honked, and all types of animals lined the streets, and I was so happy to be in Mumbai. My room at the hostel was up a few floors, but the staff helped with the bike and gear. The staff were great, and I felt relaxed and comfortable in my private room with air-con. I chose a private room because of the bike, and all the things I had that would take up a lot of space, and my snoring, played a part too.

I met a guy, Nick, and girl, Robyn, at the hostel, and that first night we caught a tuk-tuk a couple of miles to a part of town that had a lot of small restaurants and plenty going on. We sat on a step and drank some bottled beer, then had ourselves a nice and cheap meal. Robyn was heading up to the north of India the next day, and we had to say goodbye. Nick and I went to the pictures to watch Solo: A Star Wars Story, and what an experience that was. We had to stand in the theatre while people sang the national anthem. We'd heard it was mandatory. It was also a surprise to find the film was in English. It was always good to connect with people, especially when they were like Robyn and Nick.

Getting a SIM card was not exactly straightforward. I had to write my signature many times on what seemed like reams of paper, and I had two plan options. The first included 42GB of data for just £4, and the second was a card lasting three months with 126GB of data, limited to a maximum of 1.5GB per day, for £5. I gave it some thought and then splashed out on the £5 deal.

I also went to an Apple repair shop to see if they could fix my glass as it had been far too expensive in the UK. They put it on the counter, and a couple of staff looked at it and gave me a price higher than I'd had been given in the UK. They also offered me the equivalent of about £200 for it if I wanted to sell it. That's what I got for being an early adopter of the latest-model mobile phone, and being clumsy.

I didn't take any testosterone with me from the UK on the plane, so I needed to try to find a supply in Mumbai. I had contacted the airline and others to find out if I could take it on the flight and into India, but no one seemed to know. I didn't want to get in trouble, so I didn't bother. I called into a busy pharmacy around the corner from the hostel. They could only get testosterone for injecting and no syringe. I held the bottle of testosterone they showed me, and it suddenly dawned on me why I might have had such terrible pain in my right thigh on the first day of my adventure back in the UK. The pain was in the same spot where I'd had a testosterone injection a couple of years earlier that had left me unable to walk properly for over a fortnight. It was the reason I turned away from having it injected. I decided against buying testosterone from the chemist in Mumbai. It would have meant me having to find a doctor or medical professional to inject it. I chose to see how I went without it for a while. I knew there was a chance I could end up ill, and it wouldn't be good for my spine and joints, but I was sure I'd eventually source it.

After a great couple of nights in Mumbai, it was time to leave the comfort of the hostel and start my 12-mile ride through Mumbai to the Gateway of India. The gateway was an arched monument and the place from where I planned to catch a ferry across the bay to Mandve Port.

Cycling through Mumbai was a pleasure, even though it was hot and humid with clouds of dust thick enough to slice with a knife. There were a lot of coconut sellers along the roads, so I was able to stop from time to time and have a sweet cold drink of the tastiest of coconut water. At one coconut stop I became surrounded by dozens of people, all staring at me as they pulled, tugged, and pointed at the bike with curiosity.

I later took a wrong turn and found myself down some busy back-streets lined with stalls selling all kinds of animal parts from, no doubt, all sorts of animals, as well as fruits and vegetables. There were lots of other small shops and services too, but I skipped looking for a screen for my phone there. Goats, dogs, cats and birds darted across the road as I made my way along, and an older woman stopped me and pointed at a young girl who looked to be in her late teens. Though she could have been older or younger, I had no idea.

I looked at the woman in confusion as the girl looked at me in horror. The woman then held out her hand for money and continued to point at the girl. I thought she was begging for money for the girl, but then she looked in the direction of my private parts and pointed, and my heart sank.

I tried to understand what I was experiencing. There was nobody around I felt I could speak with about it. I cycled on with my head in bits. I didn't know what else to do, and I could have been so very wrong in my thinking. I had encountered more young prostitutes in the daytime on my ride through Europe than I had ever seen in my life. It had always upset me to see young prostitutes, or any prostitutes, for that matter. I would wonder what their lives were like, and what or who drove them to do it.

Along another small street, a young boy on a bike cycled about 15 yards in front of me. I cycled behind him, and I felt he must have presumed I was heading to the main road, which I'd lost sight of, so I kept following him, and sure enough he led me out of the backstreets. That little guy changed my mood and put a big smile on my face.

I arrived at the port near the Gateway of India, only to find the boat to Mandve Port had stopped running the day before. It was close to monsoon season, and the sea was too rough for the ferries. I didn't know, but it was the same every year, and I had just missed out by one day. The day had gone so well to start with but then turned terrible for a while, but a lot of smiling, friendly people eventually made my day. For about half an hour, men took turns standing with the bike and having their pictures taken, and many more had their photos taken with me. With the ferries out, I would have to cycle about 70 miles around the bay. I stayed in a hotel that night near the Gateway of India and tried to ask some locals if they knew anyone with a boat who could take me across, but I was out of luck.

I set out after a bad night's sleep due to having far too much on my mind, and I cycled for two days through roadworks and thick dust in the air. It was so lumpy that it seemed like someone had painted the roads on the hills, and I had to push my bike up a few. I also got a little lost as I approached Mandve Port, and I couldn't work out which road to take. A guy with a large estate car stopped to ask if I was okay. He told me he would give me a lift, and suggested I stayed just up the road from the port, at Ranavali Farm House and Resort. I had a clean room there with a shower and air-con, so I had a shower and rode my bike down to the port, where the ferry would have dropped me off.

On my return to the digs, I had a fantastic meal of potato paratha, paneer masala, and the tastiest mangos I had ever had. I knew that mangoes were grown locally. So many people were selling them at the roadside or in small markets. Staff at the hotel told me it was important when buying mangos or fruit to make sure the skin was intact. No holes, not even pinpricks, because bats, monkeys and lots of other wild animals love mangoes too. A lot of animals can also carry some terrible diseases.

That night, a large group of young adult men had booked in, and they were splashing and enjoying themselves in the pool. As I passed, they stopped me, and I must have stood there for 15 minutes while they took turns taking pictures of all the others standing either side of me. It was a little fun, and I returned to my room, exhausted.

Well-rested and fed, I set out in 35°C heat and high humidity and covered 35 miles to just past Kashid by 2 p.m. I was exhausted, and I hadn't expected the roads to be like they were. I found I had to continually push the bike up small but steep hills in terrible conditions, and my spine took a real beating. I had an awful pain right down my right side through to my foot, much worse than the usual sciatic pain I had. Although I had pain in those parts of my body continually, I usually managed to cope on painkillers and by keeping the pressure off my spine. The painkillers weren't doing it for me that day, and I wasn't feeling so good, but I had to push on.

By mid-afternoon, I completely ran out of steam at a small village and decided I'd look for a room. The only place on offer had slats of wood for windows with huge gaps. There was a cold water tap on the wall in the toilet room, but no shower or sink, and the toilet was just a hole in the floor surrounded by flies. There was no air-con either, which was no surprise, but there was a wobbly ceiling fan. As for the bedding, it was just a tatty blanket over a mattress that looked more worn out than I did. But no matter the situation I usually found a plus side, and the plus side was that I didn't have to sleep in my tent in the heat.

Earlier in the day, I got a glimpse of some incredible wildlife. As I cycled along at my usual sluggish pace, I spotted a dark line on the road in the distance. The road was quite narrow at that point, and the line stretched almost the full width. The scene reminded me of being back in Australia, where I often saw snakes basking on the road. I'd try to avoid running snakes over in my car in case they wrapped around the axle and struck when a passenger got out. Whether that was possible or not I had no idea, but I always avoided running over them just in case, and I didn't want to harm them either.

As I approached that dark line that day in India, it was clear it was a big snake. I had no idea what species it was, but I had a feeling it was a cobra, so I lobbed a few small rocks at it from a safe distance until it slithered off into the bushes. A little later, I spotted a giant, grey-white monkey running to the side of me just 50 yards away. It looked to be galloping like a horse at the same speed that I was cycling, and it was quite spooky looking. I'd seen monkeys like that on documentaries and had no idea what they were. It vanished into a small forest, and I was glad it did. I thought it was going to charge at one point. I spoke with a young guy in the village about the monkey, and he shook his head and said, "Very danger, very danger."

I unpacked my gear, and I lay on the floor under the tap and self-administered a few minutes of water-boarding. I had a towel on my face and let the water pound my head. It was pure bliss. I dried off and lay on the bed under the ceiling fan I had on full speed. Just as I was feeling myself about to drift off, the electricity went off and the fan came to a stop. The heat instantly returned, and I had to go outside to see if I could catch a breeze and chat to someone about getting the power back on. A guy told me it happened all the time in the village, so I went back into the room and lay on the bed. It then came back on for just a few minutes.

I decided there was no way I could sleep in that place with the lights and fan not working during the night. There was no glass or netting in the windows, which meant there was no way of stopping bugs and other critters getting in or out. I had no intention of setting my tent up in the room either. I would have sweated to death. I thought it would be better to take my chances with cobras and dangerous monkeys. As if all that wasn't bad enough, there was also no internet in town, so I packed my gear and left.

There were so many things that had happened that day. If I'd been with someone else, we'd have laughed our heads off. But even though I had nobody to joke with, I still managed a few giggles. Trying to get moving again was hard, but I kept pushing on. I came to a street sign, and although I couldn't read the language, I imagined it translated as something like: "For those struggling in the heat and humidity and dust, warm beer one mile, cold beer six miles," and I started laughing to myself at how bonkers my mind had gone, and the things I did to humour myself. I soon found another place to stay and learned that, when a sign in English says Tropical Beach Resort, I wasn't to believe any of those words applied. It was still better than the digs in the village earlier.

The next day, I catapulted out of bed like I was on a mission. I aimed for a hotel I'd found on the internet. It was nestled in some hills and looked great, with excellent views, and I thought it would be worth the climb. I had a lovely room with solid hardwood doors and furnishings and even a large balcony looking out over a valley and river. I looked forward to the evening meal because the restaurant looked clean and well set out.

At dinner, I sat myself down at a big table and the waiter handed me a menu as thick as a magazine, containing pages full of the most delicious-looking dishes. The waiter spoke some English, and I asked if there was a different menu for me, given that I'd paid for half-board. He said there was just one menu and that I could choose anything I liked. He then stood at the side of me as I flicked through the pages and images. He asked if he could make suggestions, so I agreed. He then told me to relax, and he would organise everything.

For the next hour, I enjoyed some of the best food I'd had in a long time. When I couldn't eat anything else, which took some doing, the waiter handed me the bill for more than £20. I had a feeling he'd messed up the minute he said I could choose anything I liked. I told him I had mentioned earlier my booking included the meal, but he looked at me and pointed at the bill. I just sat there looking at him, and it eventually sunk in. He ran to the kitchen and all kinds of shouting and arguing went on, and he eventually returned with a sad face and told me it was his mistake. Hotel guests had a different menu, and I didn't have to pay. I didn't feel at all bad; I felt full and satisfied, and I slept like a baby. I tipped the waiter handsomely.

Between Kashid and Ratnagiri on the coast, I covered more than 180 miles of lumpy, bumpy, dusty roads. I stayed in a couple of beautiful and cheap guesthouses and a couple of awful ones. I met some friendly people and ate the most delicious foods, but little else happened, which was a pleasant change.

The sea was getting rougher due to the monsoon moving up the coast, and fishing was hard for the locals. It was so choppy and wild, that at no point along the coast did I locate a spot where I could safely swim.

My ride in India had been tough going and a far cry from Europe. I was also struggling a bit with loneliness. Lots of people could speak some English, but the interaction was awkward. In Europe, I could quickly start a conversation with almost anyone. I felt the people I had met in India seemed to have more important things to do than stand gabbing with me, and they just went about their business. Even the dogs didn't give a shit.

Ratnagiri was a large town with a lot going on. As I looked for the hotel I had booked online a day earlier while making my way to the city, I passed a Domino's Pizza. I nearly fell off the bike as my head spun to look at it in disbelief. I located the hotel as quickly as I could, dropped my gear off and went straight back for a pizza. Indian food was lovely, but it was stodgy, high-calorie junk food that I craved. I ordered a large Mexican Veggie Pizza, garlic breadsticks and a large cola. I enjoyed every bit of it.

Back at the hotel, I went online and booked a cheap hotel in Goa for a few nights situated just a few hundred yards from the sands of Calangute Beach. I thought it would be a great place to rest up and maybe make contact with some tourists and have a few beers.

I still had 170 miles to Goa from Ratnagiri, following as close to the coast as I could. The farther south I cycled, the greener the landscape became. After cycling out of Ratnagiri, I went through dense coconut plantations. Days earlier, things had seemed dry and dusty with smaller scrub-like trees, bushes and shrubs. This part of the journey was lovely and green, but it was tough going due to the road conditions and almost vertical hills. I was in no doubt it would have been much worse farther inland. Thankfully, there were lots of small ferries to get across the dozens of estuaries and river mouths along the coast.

I received news that there was a significant outbreak of Nipah virus moving up the coast from Kerala. I read that animals like bats and pigs passed it to humans. There were 11 confirmed deaths in a short time, and many more infected. The risk of tourists contracting the virus was relatively low if they were at resorts or in the bigger cities. However, budget travellers and backpackers stood a much higher chance of getting it, and the UK government had warned about travelling to southern India while there was a risk. As a bicycle tourist I was more likely to be exposed to the virus than a lot of travellers, but I wasn't overly concerned at that point.

As soon as I arrived in Goa, I made my way to the hotel I'd booked. It had been raining heavily for the last couple of days, and it was constant. The rain was great for keeping the dust down, but the puddles and water-logged ground was likely holding all sorts of germs and other nasty things.

The hotel was very basic, and I soon understood why it was so cheap. It was holiday time for local people and those around the country, and there didn't appear to be any western tourists. I hadn't seen a single one since Mumbai. I went online in the hotel, and the weather forecast was for nothing but rain for at least a couple of weeks ahead. As the thunder and lightning went on outside, I decided that with the Nipah virus getting closer, and weather forecast, I'd seen and experienced enough of India on my incredible bicycle tour. It was time to move on.

Cycling in India had been different to how I imagined it would be. I'd been there before on holiday with Sue, and we spent two fantastic weeks in Kerala at Lighthouse Beach. During our stay, we caught a train to Goa that took 15 hours and was an experience in itself. We borrowed a car from a hotel manager in Colva and drove around for a few days. We then caught the train back to Kerala and took a rice boat tour for a few days, and also hired a car and driver to take us to a wildlife reserve. But cycling solo with not a clue where I was going to stay every night or what I would encounter was hugely different from a package holiday. I, of course, knew it would be. Bicycle touring from Mumbai to Goa was an incredible experience, and no doubt it would have been even more incredible with another person.

I gave a lot of thought to what I was going to do next. I wondered if I had done enough and was ready to go home. After about a minute of umming and ahhing, I decided I was far from ready to end my adventure. I roughly plotted a massive, almost 4,000-mile loop in South-East Asia that I would tweak as I went. I thought it would be great to fly from Goa to Bangkok in Thailand, then cycle across the Khorat Plateau in the north-eastern region to Vientiane in Laos. From there, I'd cycle down to

Cambodia, cross Cambodia and make my way through Vietnam and the Mekong Delta to the coast. I'd then cycle around the Gulf of Thailand to Surat Thani, before crossing overland to Krabi and Ao Nang.

I took a little ride down to a rocky outcrop on the coast to think a bit more. I thought about how massive the plan was. I felt I would need everything I had, mentally and physically, to complete it, and both of those things were limited.

It was easy to create a vague plan. The loop seemed to flow in my mind. I hadn't even looked at roads at that point, just the direction I hoped to travel. I was well aware it could all change at any moment, as it often did, but as soon as I could visualise the route it was a done deal, and I could think of little else. I was aware it was also the rainy season in South-East Asia. I'd heard that the rainy season in Thailand was not at all like India's. There would still usually be plenty of hours in a day that I could cycle.

I took a taxi to the airport in Goa to book my flight and found the airlines were a rip-off. I went between Jet Airways and Air India. I wanted a price for a boxed bike weighing as much as 60 pounds with the box, and 65lb of baggage, not counting hand baggage. Jet wanted £240 for the flight, and Air India wanted £220, with both changing planes at Mumbai. That was just the flights and was cheap, but it was with the baggage that the problem started. Jet demanded £500 for the bags and bike, and Air India estimated £300. They also both insisted they couldn't sell me a ticket unless I had proof of onward travel from Thailand or a return ticket back to India. To get a return ticket back to India, I had to also have an India visa for the return.

Thankfully, the visa I had bought in the UK was for multiple-entry to India, so I booked with Air India. I told them I wouldn't need to pay for the extra baggage for the return trip. The luggage wasn't returning, and neither was I. I could have booked a cheap flight out of Thailand to Lao or Vietnam as proof of my leaving Thailand. But it only cost a little more to get the return to India.

I then needed to find a bike box and pack everything up, so I took a taxi to a bike shop in Panaji, and they gave me a large, sturdy, cardboard bike box. It was the biggest they had, but it didn't look anywhere near as big as the box I was given in Turkey. I didn't need to worry, though, as I managed to squeeze the bike in after taking it apart in my hotel room.

The hotel manager booked a van to take me to the airport the following day, and a load of guys and I shared some betel nuts and paan that evening at the hotel to celebrate. Betel nuts are seeds from a type of palm tree, and a sort of stimulant drug, from what I had read. A lot of people were chewing the stuff, so I gave it a try. The guys said that paan was something similar and I should try it. My jaw was aching due to constantly chewing, and I felt no sensation. The guys were laughing as I chewed, waiting for me to lose my mind at any time. Had they known I'd lost my mind years before, they probably wouldn't have offered.

I arrived at the airport early to sort everything out, and my flight was due to leave at 11 a.m. I had never had so many upgrades in my life, but a business class seat it was. I wasn't having it that I looked smart and like business class material, but I certainly wasn't going to stand there arguing! It was only a short flight from Goa to Mumbai, but it was a treat none the less. Sadly, I only had extra legroom in economy class from Mumbai to Bangkok, which was designed for people with extra-long legs and not those of us who are extra chunky. I was so excited about arriving in Bangkok, and I felt it was going to be a massive adventure that would test me like nothing else.

CHAPTER 9

Old Bill on my case

It was June 13, 2018, when I arrived at Suvarnabhumi Airport in Bangkok, eleven months after cycling out of Warrington on that dull and wet August morning.

My first job after collecting the bike was to acquire a SIM card, which was super easy due to all the small booths competing with each other in the terminal. I simply went to the one with the longest queue, applying the same logic as I would with the busiest restaurant.

There were no shuttle buses to the hotel that I'd booked online, so I asked a taxi driver if he could get me another driver with a car more substantial than his saloon. He said there weren't any, but my bike box would fit no problem, so we fought like the Chuckle Brothers until we eventually succeeded. I was dripping in sweat, with my face almost against the windscreen. The driver was as dry as a bone and had a cocky smile from ear to ear. I was just happy to know I was heading to the hotel with all my gear.

An hour after landing in Bangkok, I was in my digs, showered, and trying to get in the mood to start the unpackalypse and build the bike. I knew it would take me a long time to sort everything out, but I felt the next time the bike would need boxing would be many months away. I was itching to get outside and start exploring, so I put the bike together and took the box to the rubbish bins and went for a ride.

The smell of food cooking was so thick in the air that I could feel myself putting more weight on. I passed a young man who had a small stall and was cooking something with eggs that looked like pancakes. I cycled past a couple of times, slowly, taking in how clean his stall was. He was making a couple of the pancake-looking things for a young girl, so I stopped and ordered two, then asked what they were. He told me they were roti. They didn't look like Indian roti and were delicious, and they instantly became my favourite street food. He fried batter on a hotplate thinly and cracked an egg on it, and when cooked, condensed milk was drizzled on it, followed by a sprinkling of sugar.

After a good sleep and with the bike and gear ready to go, I took everything downstairs to the reception area and had a huge breakfast. I then started cycling north from Bangkok towards Phra Nakhon Si Ayutthaya, which was roughly 50 miles away. It was hot and humid, but it felt much better than in India. There were light rain showers and some heavy bouts from time to time. It was their rainy season, after all, so I expected to get a little wet. I just stopped when the rain got too heavy and put up my umbrella. I covered a lot of distance that first day and one of the reasons for doing that was because it was so exciting. My mind kept busy trying to take everything in around me, including the colours, smells, people, and so many beautiful temples. Another reason for the long day was that I couldn't figure out what hotels looked like or where to find them. I just kept cycling and knew I'd spot one eventually.

Later in the day, it was time for me to act out the international sign for, "I'm bloody shattered and need to crash out." I put my two palms together and tucked my hands under the side of my head and closed my eyes. It worked, and someone eventually directed me to some digs for £17 for a lovely air-conditioned room, including breakfast. The first thing I noticed from the outside of the hotel was a sign with 24/7 and Wi-Fi. That was how I was going to locate places to stay, I thought

I enjoyed my first day, but I had a little blood running down my leg at one point from sores. I had bought some short, padded cycling shorts when I was back in the UK, and it was the first time I tried a pair under my regular shorts. I thought they'd fit by the time I got to Thailand, but nope, I was still the same weight. I'd lost a bit on the way to Valencia in Spain, but once my body had adjusted to doing the same thing day in day out, and I got used to rewarding myself with beer at the end of most days, my weight went back up. The new shorts lifted right up between my legs and between my butt cheeks like a thong, chafing and sawing away. On the plus side, my legs felt three inches longer.

My second day was great too, as I managed to get away from the busier roads and onto back roads along rivers and canals. I found a roadside water machine costing pennies, so I filled the bottles. While straddling the bike, I read about the coolers on the internet and learned that they were okay at best and lethal at worst. They didn't filter out viruses and were said to be poorly maintained or not maintained at all. Suddenly, and while drinking from one of the bottles, I felt pain in my left leg, like ants biting in multiple places, so I looked down and found my foot firmly planted in a nest of red ants. Halfway through the day, I took shelter from the heat in a tiny roadside restaurant, where I ditched the machine water in favour of cold bottled water. I heard that lots of people used the machines, but as it was only pennies for bottled water, I chose not to risk it.

As I cycled towards Saraburi and onto some small back roads, people I passed smiled and waved, and it was lovely. There were times when it was necessary to cycle on the bigger roads, but even they had lots of little shops and places to eat, and the highways had shoulders of at least gravel. I would have felt quite safe if it wasn't for motorbikes and scooters coming down the shoulder towards me on the wrong side of the road. The problem with them coming down the hard shoulder was they would keep as far away from the lanes as they could, forcing me closer to the traffic. I wasn't having any of it, so I always tried to make sure it was them who were closer to the vehicles. They didn't like it, but I didn't care; I had my own life to consider.

The food during the first couple of days was great; cheap and tasty dishes created at the roadside in little makeshift kitchens, some the size of small garden sheds. Hotels were very affordable, and my second night north of Saraburi was just under £10. I had air-con, a shower, double bed, room for the bike, and ants - tiny little ants, all over the fridge and even in the bed. After paying for the room, the management vanished. I tried to ignore the ants as they weren't biters, but after trying to focus on my laptop screen for an hour with dozens of tiny ants crawling all over it as I lay in bed, I had to get some ant killer. There were 7-Eleven shops everywhere, and their air-con was super cold. I would often stop at them to get out of the heat and have an iced coffee. Back from the 7-Eleven and armed with the ant killer, I emptied half the can in the room.

Before long I arrived in Nakhon Ratchasima, high on the Khorat Plateau in the Isan region of north-east Thailand. Wow; all that I just wrote sounded so exotic. It was a bit of a climb to get onto the plateau, and there were a few hills to navigate right after, but the approach to Nakhon Ratchasima flattened out quite a bit.

Once in the city, I popped into a bike shop. Since arriving in Thailand, my rear brake hadn't been working correctly. There appeared to be little in the way of brake fluid for some reason. It could have been that the bike box was upside down on the flight and could have lost fluid as a result, or that the brakes were just due for a service. Beaze Bob Bike Shop staff got straight to work while I had a cup of coffee from their little inside café. After repairing the brakes, they asked if they could take a photo of me with the shop in the background. I cycled off, and the brakes felt great. A great job and excellent service and I couldn't thank them enough. They didn't even charge me.

According to the forecast for the week ahead, it was going to be 34°C, feeling like 40°C. It was hard going in such heat and humidity. Thankfully, the roads were in fantastic condition everywhere, and I covered a lot of highway miles. I loved being on the busier roads from time to time, as there were often people I could interact with, even if we couldn't speak each other's languages. I would get a little lonely when I didn't have a proper conversation in person with anyone for days on end.

I estimated it would take me at least four or five days to reach Vientiane in Laos from Nakhon Ratchasima, or even a week. I was really in no rush. Once there, I planned to have a few days off in the city to gather some strength before cycling south alongside the Mekong River, and I couldn't wait to see the river. I had a thing for big rivers for some strange reason, and I had loved being in the Brazilian Amazon and on the Amazon River system for my 40th birthday. Maybe it was the strength and power or the abundance of wildlife, and all the places or countries that big rivers flowed through. I had no idea what to expect from the Mekong River, but I was excited all the same.

I was following the Mittraphap Road to Laos, which was one of Thailand's longest highways. It was busy but there wasn't much in the way of wind, and I shoved an earphone in my verge-side ear and listened to mellow songs. After a long, hot day in the saddle, I found a guesthouse on the map, but it meant an eight-mile detour. It was the only place to stay I could find, but I would have to cycle eight miles back to the highway the next morning.

On arrival, I was surprised to find that the district of Phimai was much bigger than I thought. There was also an incredible temple complex known as Phimai Historical Park, home to one of largest Khmer temples outside of Cambodia. After settling into my digs, I went over to take a closer look at the temples, and I wasn't disappointed. The park reminded me of all the photos I'd seen of Angkor Wat in Cambodia, which was on my bucket list. I then took a trip to the town's centre to find some food. I met a couple of English gents at a bar, and we chatted and had a few beers. A little while later, a South African lady teacher and another lady from Australia joined us. So it was more beer and chats, and I enjoyed it.

Back when I was in the UK after Turkey, I didn't know it at that time, but on my last day, I went through a speed trap at three miles over the speed limit. I had to pay the fine of £100 online and write a letter to the Cheshire Constabulary to accept responsibility. I only had myself to blame, of course. I wasn't aware of the speeding issue until I'd left Phimai and received an email from Sue saying she'd had a letter arrive at home. I felt a little down about having points on my licence. They were my first.

At the end of a hot and dusty day on Mittraphap Road, I called into some offices that delivered parcels and letters. I used two different translation apps on my phone to try to communicate. But my miserable attempts resulted in blank stares from some, and giggles from others. I tried to use an image from my phone of a letter with a stamp on it, and I even picked up one of their envelopes from a table and expressed in the best way I could that I wanted to send my own. From a room of about 15 people, I got nothing at all back, which I thought was weird. The teacher back in Phimai had told me it was tough to teach English in that region. She said that for a new face in town, it wouldn't matter if they could talk to local people in their language fluently; the locals wouldn't get past the fact they were foreigners, and so wouldn't understand what they were saying.

I found what the teacher said a bit strange, and I doubted that was the case at the time. But after trying to get my message across to such a large group of people, I started to believe it. I couldn't get help finding or buying envelopes or notepads either. The offices happened to be next door to a hotel, so I booked in and asked at reception if I could print a letter on the printer that was behind their desk. I wanted to send an email to the hotel so they could print it out for me. After about 15 minutes of trying to explain, I gave up and went to my room, and after a shower and a cup of instant noodles, I was out like a light. My brain felt like it had been a piñata at a party for unruly children.

During the next few days, I managed to find a children's notepad that needed cropping a little and even some envelopes at a 7-Eleven. I located a post office too, where I took a ticket and sat waiting patiently. I then handed over two letters. One letter was addressed to the police, and the other to my wife, just in case the one to the police didn't make it. If the police said they hadn't received it, which I thought was entirely possible, then Sue would send or deliver the other copy in person.

I was approaching Khon Kaen, which was 280 miles from Bangkok, and the temperature was off the scale. Cycling the highway had its plusses, but it also had its downsides. Cycling a long road with barely a turn for days was hard work at times. I would often feel I wasn't getting anywhere. I had my sights set on Vientiane, so having a goal kept me moving. Shops and petrol stations were numerous, and I was at least able to stop regularly to get cold drinks and to rest. Although shops and services lined the highway, they didn't always line both sides on the same stretch. South of Khon Kaen, I cycled for many miles where all the petrol stations, including 7-Elevens and shops, were on the opposite side, separated from me by ditches and a barrier. I was unable to get a drink or cool down without a lot of hard work. It was pure torture trying to keep my tongue from getting tangled in the back wheel.

It was soon time to hit the big city of Khon Kaen, and I was looking forward to finding familiar foods like burgers and pizzas. I was sick of noodles, rice, and soup, and I needed a high-calorie, stodgy pig-out.

After 30 miles in heat and dust, I entered the city to a banging and clanging from the rear wheel: I had my first broken spoke. It had snapped clean off close to the hub. I located a hotel named Tonwa Resort, which was just a mile away, so I hobbled on, hoping I wouldn't lose another spoke. I was surprised at how loud the noise of a spoke breaking was, and how instantly I developed a wobble.

What I should have done before hobbling to the digs was tie or tape the broken spoke to another spoke to stop it swinging loose, but I didn't, and on my arrival at Tonwa Resort, the spoke was bent all over the place. I was lucky it hadn't caused more damage. After settling into a great room at the hotel, I had the spoke replaced and the wheel trued in no time, and I was quite proud of myself. Another thing I did on one of my short trips back to the UK was to go on a wheel building and truing course for a day with BikeRight in Liverpool. Coincidentally, a guy I was with on the training course happened to be following my adventure on social media. He thought that what I was doing was incredible, which was nice.

Back when I had that bulging tyre and wobble in France, I thought then how knowing how to true a wheel would be an essential skill. The course was great, and the skills I learned in just one day finally came in handy, as I knew they would. I had plenty of spare spokes in two different sizes because those on the rear wheel were much shorter than those on the front. The size of the hub made the difference, and the shorter spokes added strength to the rear wheel. I also had a great little toolkit I'd put together after reading about all the problems I stood a chance of having.

While checking in, the hotel receptionist gave me a bag of what looked like manky tomatoes. They turned out to be the tastiest of oranges, and I ate the lot while repairing the wheel.

After a wash and change of clothes, I cycled over to a McDonald's on the highway and stuffed my face like a hamster. After prising myself out of the restaurant like a cork from a wine bottle, I noticed my little rubber tyrannosaurus mascot, Rex, had vanished. He was about five inches long and fastened to my handlebars. I had found the little guy almost broken in two at the side of a road months earlier, and we had become good friends. He was my Wilson, from the Tom Hanks film Cast Away, and it was quite sad to find him gone. But the sadness vanished just minutes later when I found Gordon on the road as I made my way back to the hotel. He was a sorry-looking rubber gecko covered in dust and dirt, so I cleaned him up, and he fit perfectly in the same spot on my handlebars where the late Rex had been. I felt he would be an excellent new companion.

As I left Khon Kaen, I estimated I had two reasonably short days, followed by a long day, to reach Friendship Bridge. The bridge spanned the mighty Mekong River. Once across, I planned to follow the Mekong on the Laos side until the town of Thakhek. From there I hoped to cross back over to Thailand at Nakhon Phanom.

On the very long road on the incredible plateau, I discovered little clusters of huts or self-contained units that were known as resorts. I'd passed some of them shortly after leaving Bangkok, but I couldn't work out what they were. A day before Khon Kaen, I called into a resort to ask what it was, because that one had 24/7 and Wi-Fi written on a sign out front. The small buildings were in rows, and I found out later they were mostly on the busier roads, and were used by truck drivers and people who wanted a place to go for an hour or two for all sorts of reasons. The owner of the resort gave me one of the small buildings that had a shower room with a toilet and sink. I had no neighbours attached and was also able to wheel the bike inside. It had a double bed, air-con, television, and a small table with chairs. It was worth every penny of £10, and I was hooked and would make sure to look out for them.

As Vientiane neared, I met a couple of great guys: John, from Blackpool, and a petrol station manager. I couldn't work out the manager's name, but he was super friendly. He saw me cycle out of his petrol station and jumped in his car to catch up with me and pulled in front and handed me a bottle of water and some sticky rice cooked in bamboo. Both of those guys made my day.

A couple of resort hotels later, it was time to cycle over Friendship Bridge into Laos, and it felt incredible. I had cycled 400 miles of some fantastic landscape and smiling people. On my approach to the immigration buildings a European-looking guy at a café gave me a wave, and I waved back. I didn't know it at the time, but I would meet that guy again.

Passing through immigration was smooth, and I had a laugh with the Thai border guards, and one of them gave me some bananas and a bottle of water. I wasn't sure at first whether or not I would be allowed on the bridge with the bike, because it was only one lane each way with no shoulder, but I had no problems.

The Laos border control was nothing like Thailand's. There was a lot of messing about with my paperwork, scowls, looks up and down and pointing. In Laos, everything seemed instantly different. The streets were in bad condition, and traffic appeared disorderly. The smiles I was so used to in Thailand were also few and far between in Laos. But it was the tenth country on my adventure. It was also the fifth on my ride I had never been to before. It was hard to believe I had cycled from Bangkok, and it felt great.

I found some rather posh digs in Vientiane, and although not cheap, the staff at Vayakorn Inn kept my bike inside near the reception desk. I tried about six other hotels first, including a couple of hostels, but all wanted me to leave my bike outside. I booked the hotel for two nights because I wanted to make more of an effort to take rest days from cycling. It had taken me ten days to cycle from Bangkok to Vientiane and, considering the heat and humidity, and the fact I was a little sluggish, that was good going. It wasn't easy to find a SIM card in the city, but after an hour or so of walking around town, I found one in a little deli-style shop.

I was up early on my first full day in Vientiane and thought it was a city that could have eventually grown on me, but it would have taken a very long time. It was okay, but there was just something about it I didn't like, and I couldn't put my finger on what. It was a busy city, and there were a lot of tourists, and I heard it was a place where many backpackers and travellers liked to renew their Thai visas.

It was hard for me to relax and stay in one spot when on my own. With other people, I would have had a giggle, but on my own, I often found myself just pottering about trying to think of something to do, which was why I rarely took rest days. I knew I had to rest at times, especially to try to heal my butt and cure a few sores, but I struggled with it.

I decided to go on the hunt for noodle soup because I'd heard it was extra tasty in Laos. The first place I tried was heaving with local people. It was small and run-down, but I thought it had to be worth a go with it being so popular.

Just as I was about to tuck into my pork noodle soup, a cockroach decided it wanted to share it with me. It shuffled across the table with what looked like a couple of broken legs. The table then jolted for some reason, and I grabbed my bowl. The cockroach just stood, lopsided and looking right at me, so I gave it a flick, right between its beady eyes. It hit the wall with such a smack that the people on the next table turned to see what the noise was. I then surprised myself by still eating all of the soup, which was one of the tastiest noodle soups I'd had. Lunch and the cockroach entertainment came to about £1.50, including a small bottle of water. The next place I tried, a few hours later, charged me about £2.50 for the same sort of soup, but my first soup was tastier and meatier, for reasons I could only imagine.

Later that day I met a guy named Justin, who was in the city for a week on business before returning to Perth, Australia, where he lived. Having lived there myself, and travelled there many times, we chilled and shared a few stories over beers and pizza in the evening.

The next morning, it was chucking it down, and the forecast was for heavy rain for a couple of days, then showery weather for the rest of the week. I wasn't in much of a rush to get soaking wet, so I decided to stay at the hotel a little longer. I was okay with being cosy and having lots of bars and restaurants within walking distance.

While walking along some of the busy roads near the hotel, I passed a Brazilian steakhouse, and while having a great meal there later that day, I changed my plans for the days ahead. I decided to cross back over the Friendship Bridge and follow the Mekong down to Nakhon Phanom on the Thai side, and then on to Mukdahan - a total of around 300 miles. I thought I'd then head to Ubon Ratchathani, and from there, I hadn't a clue. I did like the thought of cycling through a wildlife sanctuary or two on my way to Cambodia, though.

Regarding visas, sadly the one I had for Thailand was single-use, meaning if I wanted to go back into Thailand, I needed to get another visa in Laos. I could have got a short visa at the border for a couple of weeks at most, but that wouldn't have been long enough. So I decided to go to the Embassy of Thailand in Vientiane and get a three-month visa. I thought I'd only need about two or three weeks to reach Cambodia, but didn't want to have to rush, so I went for a three-month, single-entry visa. It was the safer option. I could never really be sure what I would get up to from one minute to the next.

Trying to find the embassy was tough going on my bike. I kept getting lost or turning up at the wrong place, but I eventually located it. At the gates, one of the guards told me I couldn't take my bike inside the compound area. He looked pretty sleepy and was tucked away in his box outside the embassy gates. As there wasn't anything to lock the bike to, I put my lock cable around his telephone cable. The telephone cable went from somewhere inside the compound and into the guard's tiny box, which was no bigger than a small garden shed. I thought nobody would be able to steal the bike without either cutting the telephone cable or alerting the guard. In the embassy, I had to fill out an application and take it back the following morning. On exiting, I could have died. The guard had left, and my bike was alone on the footpath of a busy road. He'd passed his phone and cable through my lock cable and just left the bike for anyone to take. It was my fault. I should have cycled back to the hotel and caught a cab back to the embassy.

I settled in at the hotel and called Sue for a chat. I'd managed to phone her most days using WhatsApp or Facebook Messenger, free of charge. She told me she'd been in contact with the police regarding the points on my licence and asked them if they'd received my letter. She hadn't received the one I sent her. Not only had the police not received my letter, but they also said it wouldn't be accepted anyway. I'd need to download and sign a form, then post it to the police in an envelope because an electronic copy like an email attachment would not be accepted. They also wanted me to send my driving licence. They said if they didn't receive the documents within two weeks, the matter would go to the courts. If I failed to return to the UK to attend court, an arrest was likely.

It was three points! I wasn't a robber or vicious criminal. I had no choice but to download the form and fill it out, which I managed to do the next morning. There was no way I was posting my licence, especially after two previous letters went missing. I downloaded two copies of the form, one for the police and one for Sue. I could have done without all the messing. It was a distraction I didn't need, but it was my fault for speeding. I'd have never forgiven myself if I'd harmed someone.

It was soon time to get back over to the embassy to collect my passport and visa.

CHAPTER 10

Unbelievable panty-liners

My visa was approved, and I was soon cycling out of Laos and starting my journey along the Mekong River. I decided to stay the night in Nong Khai, a Thai province next to the Mekong River. It's popular with British expats and other Europeans, and just a 16-mile ride from my hotel in Vientiane.

I needed to allow some time to get across the border into Thailand and sort out some mail. Once across Friendship Bridge, I located a post office and told the staff I wanted my letters sent the best way possible. It cost me £30, but I was desperate for the letters to get to their destinations. I then booked into digs, had a cold shower, and changed into some clean clothes. I took a little trip over to a bar and met some friendly expats. One of the guys asked if I remembered him. It turned out he was the guy who had waved to me as I approached Friendship Bridge on my way to Laos some days earlier.

After a good sleep, it was time to get moving along the river and, for roughly 30 miles, I cycled some fabulous roads and a very long cycle path to Phon Phisai. I couldn't understand why there was such a great cycle path in an area where there wasn't much around. I could only presume they were planning for well into the future. It was a beautiful part of Thailand.

The forecast for the week ahead was hot and humid, as usual, but with thunderstorms and heavy rain in the afternoon. So, after just another 30 miles the next day, I arrived at the KongKhamKoon Hotel, near Pak Khat, and it wasn't even lunchtime. I was in no rush in the crazy heat, and I wanted to make time to wander around the town and along the river. My room had a huge bath, so I filled it with cold water and dived in at the deep end, then lay in it for about an hour until I started to feel cold. While in the bath, the heavens opened, so I sat on the balcony looking out across the beautiful Mekong River to the hills of Laos on the other side.

For me, it was always worth spending a little extra money for a great location. Not that I didn't enjoy camping - I did - but I had no intention of camping in Thailand because hotels and other places to stay were so cheap. Not only that, but the thought of sleeping in a tent in the bushes somewhere on my own in the rainy season in such heat and high humidity, with all kinds of weird critters crawling over and under my tent all night, didn't seem appealing.

Once the rain eased, I went out and did a bit of shopping. I bought a few beers, of course, and visited the Pak Khat District Municipal Food Market, which was incredible. I purchased some deep-fried chicken pieces and potato balls. The chicken pieces had been cooked and put on a rack, so I asked the two young girls serving to drop them back in the hot oil for a minute. There were all kinds of live animals for sale, such as turtles and snails, and dozens of species of fish. I tried to film some of the live fish in large buckets, but people glared at me, and some buckets were quickly covered up. On leaving the market, I bought two banana-filled roti for dessert. I put all the food and beer on a table on my hotel porch and enjoyed the view. I then fell asleep to the sounds of a couple of geckos behind the curtains.

The next morning, I cruised along some lovely smooth, undulating roads, and the forests appeared to be turning to dense jungle. Later in the day, I called into a chemist in Bueng Kan, near where I had booked into a hotel. I wanted to try out an idea I had to ease my saddle sores and abrasions, which continued to haunt me. I thought that, at some point, I would have developed some hard skin or thick calluses. Sadly, I hadn't, and it may have been down to the sticky heat and humidity and my constant sweating keeping the sores open. I picked up some female panty-liners, with wings, and asked the staff if they were the largest size they had. One lady handed me a different pack and started laughing, and the others laughed too. I led the ladies to the door of the shop where I'd parked the bike, and I pointed to the saddle and tried to explain I wanted to wrap the panty-liners around it. Communication was difficult, but it eventually clicked with one of them, and she told the others. It was a funny situation.

I opened the packet when I got back to the hotel, and I could have died. They were massive, and it was no wonder the ladies were laughing. God only knew who or what they were supposed to fit. But they wrapped around the saddle, and then some, so I was good to give it a go.

After some cold beers and a comfortable night, I was up early and raring to hit the road, and I stuck a couple of panty-liners to my inner thighs for good measure. After a couple of hours of near painless cycling, I thought I was onto something. By mid-afternoon, the panty-liners on my thighs had sweated off and were just two soggy lumps in my shorts. The ones on the saddle were still stuck but weren't soft, and my butt had started to hurt again. The landscape that day was beautiful and it helped to take my mind off my arse, which was then as sore as it had ever been. It was a real pleasure to cycle the undulating, twisty roads and thick forest around Phu Wua Wildlife Sanctuary, home to more than 40 wild elephants. I read that there were also bears and tigers, and leopards, but I had no idea if that was true or not. I would have loved to have seen the wild elephants, but I was out of luck. I thought they might have smelled me before I got a whiff of them, but there was one point when I was sure they were close. The smell was so strong. I just stood there straddling the bike as still as I could, while looking deep into the forest to see if I could see them, but I only heard twigs snapping. I later crossed paths with two small snakes, and one of them tried to bite my tyre.

After a great rest that evening, I decided the next day I would force myself to eat some food from some small roadside eateries. I had gone off eating like that due to concerns over hygiene. I had never had a problem with street food until I started my bicycle adventure. Flying into a country and walking around a town eating whatever was on offer at the roadside was always a highlight of my regular holidays. But on the bicycle I would see how some people who cooked the food lived, and I witnessed food preparation. I saw animals hanging from trees and other ingredients in buckets in the open air, covered in flies at times.

I turned to simple foods that were deep-fried in hot oil in front of me or cooked on a hot plate or grill, and I always felt safe with roti. I also stayed clear of fish and shellfish. Fish farming was widespread, but the conditions were often not regulated or not regulated well. I avoided prawns because the chance of those critters coming from the ocean and not a farm was slim at best. I couldn't afford to have a bad stomach while cycling all day, so I usually opted for foods in sealed packaging, like biscuits, bread and instant noodles, and beer. Not the healthiest of foods, but I felt sure I wouldn't get ill or a dicky tummy with it.

So I sat down in a tiny restaurant at lunchtime, and without even seeing a menu, a plate of boiled rice with chicken and a bowl of what looked like chicken stock landed on the table. I thought it must have just been the meal of the day, all day, every day. I saw other people eating the same food, and it was quite tasty for about £1. I later called into another small establishment and had pork fried rice with a fried egg on top. The egg had a nasty, unhealthy odour to it, like roadkill, so I put the egg to one side and ate everything else, even though I could still smell the egg. I was fully aware my stomach wasn't capable of eating like the locals; some of them must have had stomachs like crocodiles. I had given the small roadside restaurants another try, and I was back to sealed packaging, fried foods and beer. Beer was so cheap out there, and I rarely went a day without a bottle or two. I hardly ever drank beer at home.

The next morning, I set out early at 6.30 a.m. with just a bottle of water, and I was hungry. About an hour later, I managed to buy a couple of yoghurts and a coffee from a small shop. I tried to stay as close to the Mekong River as I could because the views across to Laos were breathtaking. It was great being on the more minor roads in those parts, as I met lots of local people who wanted to interact with me. I came across some people picking what looked like some sort of fruit from a tree. The fruits were about an inch across, so I stopped and smiled at the people and showed an interest in what they were doing, in the hope of trying whatever it was. A guy brought one of the fruits over to me and removed the peel with a big black fingernail, which looked frightfully clean afterwards. He handed the almost translucent, gelatinous-looking flesh to me to eat, and I couldn't say no. It was so tasty, and I smiled and nodded, and then a lady came over to me and gave me a large bunch of about 50 to take with me. It was lovely of them. I parked up about a mile later and ate the lot while looking up the fruit on the internet. It was longan, common in the north of Thailand, and from the Lamyai tree.

After a good feed, I cycled on and came across a tiny bridge on the outskirts of a small village. I was just about to cross when out popped about eight soldiers carrying rifles. They blocked the road and flagged me down, then approached me with stern expressions. I stood still and watched as they employed the Zulu impis bullhorn tactic to work their way around me. Without warning, a soldier who stood in front of me took a photo of us with his phone. We all had a bit of a laugh before they waved me on.

After another great sleep in more cheap-but-comfortable digs, I felt fit and ready for anything. Not long into my ride, while I was taking a break, the rear stand fell off my bike. Small bolts that held it on had snapped, and the bike fell on its side, with no damage to the bike or bags. I cycled through a small town a little while later and saw some guys working on a motorbike. They had a load of tools scattered across the floor, so I asked if any spoke English. None did, so I held out my stand and pointed at where it should have been on the bike. They got straight to it and put two new bolts in, and I was good to go. I gave them the equivalent of about £10 and thanked them.

A few miles farther along and I felt the rear wheel sliding. I had developed a slow puncture just three miles from a resort I had seen on the map.

I tried to ride on but I didn't get very far, and across the road from where I had stopped was a petrol station and what looked like a large restaurant with windows. Windows usually meant air-con, so I dumped the bike outside the door of the restaurant and plonked my butt down at a table. I received a menu, which was a real treat, but it was in Thai with no images. I pointed to a table where two hungry men were elbow-deep in what looked like bowls of meaty noodle soup. I said to the waitress, "I want that one," just how Andy Pipkin from Little Britain would have said it. It was clear she hadn't watched Little Britain, but she smiled and nodded and vanished into the kitchen. A few minutes later a fantastic beef noodle soup arrived, along with salad and loads of condiments. It was delicious.

I then had to get to work fixing the puncture. A police officer based at the petrol station was kind enough to lend me a hand and some company. His English was excellent, so I was able to share a few funny stories. As we were talking, two young women walked by, and one of them pointed at the other and told us she needed a husband, and we all started laughing. Puncture repaired, the officer gave me a cold bottle of water, and a few minutes later, I was in my digs. The hotel sign read Private Place in Thai, and it was in Tha Uthen District, just north of Nakhon Phanom.

The next day, I cycled towards Nakhon Phanom, and just four miles into my ride I again got a flat tyre. I hadn't been on the road very long, and I was sweating profusely in the humidity. Right across the street, there was a large industrial compound and lots of shady trees over a parking area, which looked like an ideal spot to change a tube. But within minutes, I was turfed out of the grounds for some reason by angry employees. Right next door to the compound was a motorbike repair shop, where the owner and I set about sorting the problem. I didn't need the help, of course, but he wanted to, and it was a little company for me. There must have been a wire strand or something thin sticking through the tyre that I couldn't find. I wouldn't usually have a couple of punctures so close together.

In Nakhon Phanom, I bought a cheap 700x32 tyre at a small bike shop. It wasn't a great make of tyre, and it was expensive at £20. No doubt the shop owner saw me coming. I wasn't hard to miss, after all. I installed the new tyre on the front wheel and put the wider Marathon Supreme from the front on the rear. I also managed to buy five spare tubes and a puncture repair kit at the shop for £22. I rarely tried to repair an inner tube. I wasn't very good at it and preferred to dump them and replace them with new ones. Before I bought the bike, I'd read so many articles advising people to avoid wheels over 26 inches. Some believed it would have been hard to find tyres and tubes to fit a larger rim in a lot of countries. I knew little about bikes at the time, but I doubted that was the case. I thought it might have been the case many years before 700 became popular, so I went for larger wheels, and I was glad I did. I had no trouble at all getting hold of tyres and tubes. If my plan had been to cycle mostly very rough terrain, I'd have probably gone for 26s, because I felt shorter spokes and smaller rims would have been much more robust. Another reason I didn't want smaller wheels was that I didn't like the look of them on a large frame.

I booked into a resort run by an elderly couple for the night. After a shower and sorting out my gear in my super little self-contained hut, I popped to the reception and asked the elderly lady for a couple of beers. She looked at me and couldn't understand what I was saying, so I pointed to the fridge that had stickers of two popular beers on it, Chang and Leo, and I acted out drinking beer. She said I could have a different room if I wanted company. I told her I didn't want that, and pointed again at the fridge and said "Chang Leo." I started to walk away, but she told me to wait. She got on the phone and started talking to someone in Thai. After passing the phone over to me, an English-speaking lady asked what time I wanted a woman. I told her I didn't want a woman. I just wanted a beer. She started laughing and said her mum had misunderstood. I handed the phone over to her mum, and she started laughing when her daughter explained, and I started laughing. She then went over to the fridge and got some beer. I asked for four. I'd originally only wanted two, but after all that, I needed more.

I was up early the next day to put in some miles and was on the road for 6 a.m. and on my way to That Phanom. It was a lovely day. I found a tidy waterfront resort and had some great food at a restaurant. While finishing my meal, the restaurant staff told me they were closing because they were going for something to eat. I wondered at first what was wrong with the food there, but understood that nobody liked eating in the same place or eating the same food all the time. Back in the UK, fish and chips and western foods were great, but now and then I liked an Indian or Chinese. At least I hoped it was a similar reason to why they were eating somewhere else.

After being turfed out of the restaurant, I went for a walk around the town. I came across a temple I wanted to return to in daylight, so I went to bed and was out like a light. I was at the temple, Wat Phra That Phanom, early in the morning, and there was hardly a soul around.

The route I had taken through Thailand wasn't the most popular with bicycle tourists. I hadn't seen a single one since arriving in Thailand weeks before. The attractions were terrific but few and far between on the plateau. From what I had experienced of the Khorat Plateau, I viewed it as the breadbasket of Thailand. Or rice basket, because I hadn't seen wheat or grains growing anywhere. I'd read blogs from other bicycle tourists who had cycled from Bangkok to Chiang Mai, or Chiang Mai to Lao, or from Bangkok to Phuket or Malaysia. Another popular route appeared to be from Bangkok to Siem Reap in Cambodia. I didn't want popular; I wanted to do something a little different, and I was so glad I did.

Early in the morning, I spent some time wandering around the grounds of Wat Phra That Phanom, and just as I was about to leave, a man came over on his bike and asked me where I was going. I told him I was heading to Mukdahan, and he asked if he could join me for half an hour. He said he rode to Mukdahan, which was roughly 50 miles, most weekends, and back home again. I welcomed the company, and it was good fun. However, he did like cycling alongside me instead of in front or behind, even when the traffic was hectic. He had my nerves gone at times, and each time a large vehicle came up behind us I'd slow down so that my buddy could get in line in front of me.

After my cycling buddy headed back, the heavens opened, and I stood under a tree with the umbrella up for about half an hour before it stopped. While taking shelter, I got to thinking about how handy it was to have flat rubber pedals. I had no experience with any other kind of pedal, and I didn't want to have to buy special shoes and use clips. I didn't like the idea of the pointy metal type either, as they would have played havoc with Crocs or bare feet. I was happy with my choice of pedals that I could wear anything or nothing with, though they did get a little slippery when wet. To combat that, I stuck a sports sock on each pedal if the bad weather was in for the day, or sometimes I would use my neoprene gloves on the pedals.

I arrived in Mukdahan late in the afternoon. From there, I had two route choices to Ubon Ratchathani, which was over 100 miles south of Mukdahan. One option was to go along the Mekong River some more before heading west, and the other was to head directly to Ubon Ratchathani, which was the shorter route. After giving it some thought, I decided to take the shortest route. I was Mekonged out, anyway.

After settling into a resort, just before heavy thunder and lightning and torrential rain began, I started feeling a little uncomfortable after a visit from the owner. The room was roughly £15, and the receptionist asked me to pay a deposit of about the same again. I was okay with that and paid. But after settling into my room, the owner came to see me and asked for a key deposit. I asked her what the deposit I'd already paid was for, and she told me I hadn't paid. After a trip to the reception desk, we managed to sort it.

I was over a week away from Cambodia at that point, and I was ready for it. I had been wandering around north-west Thailand on my own for long enough, and I needed some new scenery. I planned to make extra effort to cover longer distances each day, to make it to the Cambodian border sooner. So the next day I covered another 50 miles, which wasn't so easy in the rainy season. On arrival at a resort, I couldn't believe my luck; they had a washing service and asked me if I needed it. My clothes hadn't had a machine wash since I was back in the UK after Turkey. Not only did I get my clothes washed, but the owners of the resort brought over an ice bucket with a couple of beers.

I didn't get going until 9 a.m. the next morning due to heavy rain. But as soon as it eased off, I put on my Hock poncho and bicycle helmet with a disposable plastic shower cap over it. I was on a mission to reach

Ubon Ratchathani that day, and the rain wasn't going to hold me back. I was exhausted by the time I arrived there, but I was thrilled I had cycled just over 100 miles in two days.

I had just 115 miles left to cycle in Thailand to my next target, the Chong Chom border crossing, where I hoped to enter Cambodia. There were so many things I wanted to see in Cambodia, such as Angkor Wat and the Killing Fields. I hoped then to cycle through the heart of Ho Chi Minh City in Vietnam, then the Mekong Delta. What I'd learned from thousands of miles of cycling was that anything could happen at any time with me, and it usually did. I didn't want to raise my hopes too high at that point, because I was still a long way from the border.

Realising the poorest people have the biggest smiles

With days still to go to the Chong Chom border crossing, I met a guy on a fat bike that had a Brooks saddle, two empty rear panniers, and massive, chunky, knobbly tyres. He was going in the same direction but on his way to work, so we had a little chat, and he continued cycling and vanished over the horizon in no time at all.

After a great day of riding through an incredible landscape of rice paddies as far as the eye could see, I stopped at a hotel that had what they called a V.I.P. Room. It had a large bath, lounge chair, and big-screen TV, and the bed looked like a big slice of heaven, with white sheets and four pillows. After giving it a little thought for what must have been seconds, I pushed the boat out and paid the almost-£20 asking price. There was also a large restaurant on-site, but it wasn't open. Thankfully they still cooked the meals and provided room service at no extra charge, so I ordered a lovely chicken and cashew nut meal. I was in no doubt my living standards in Thailand would have looked a little extravagant, but compared with European prices, digs were so cheap. Most of the places I'd stayed in Thailand wouldn't have made a single star rating in Europe, but they were far more comfortable than a tent.

I sprayed bug killer all around the rooms before unpacking almost daily in Thailand, and each time I'd find dead bugs on the floor afterwards. Most digs included geckos. Early on, I wondered what the weird croaking, chirping sound was. I'd turn the lights out and the noise would start, even after fumigating the room on arrival. I thought the sounds were from giant crickets or some other sort of hardcore bug, then one night, I turned the light on and saw a gecko on the wall near the air-con unit. I could hardly make it out. It was almost the same colour as the wall and looked as thin as paper, but was about five inches long. As I approached, it darted behind the unit. I turned the light off, and it started making a racket again. The geckos were loud and annoying, and the only way I could combat them was to not sleep in the dark. They were a pain in the butt, but I liked them all the same.

On my way to Khukhan, which was just 50 miles from the border, I came across a dragon fruit seller, and I was hungry at the time. I was hungry all the time, so I bought two big ones for less than £1. I enjoyed the fresh produce at the roadsides. Back when I'd cycled to Laos there was wild honey for sale, still in the honeycomb, and it included bees that were thick in the air. Cycling down from Laos along the Mekong, other kinds of fruit and vegetables were for sale, and it was the same inland on my way to the Cambodian border. Different regions had different products for sale. I didn't know what I would come across next.

I found a great little resort just after Khukhan with about half a dozen units, styled to look like VW campervans. I cycled into the grounds, but there was nobody around. I took shelter from the rain and thunder outside the office door and kept knocking. I felt there must have been someone around. Eventually, a guy opened the office door looking half-asleep, and he apologised and led me to my unit, which was great. I always knew that I was in good digs when there were hardly any dead bugs after a spray.

My aim for the next day was to get as close to the border as I could, then get some digs on the Thai side, and cross into Cambodia the following day with plenty of energy.

Just before lunchtime the following day, I came across a durian fruit seller. I'd heard about the fruit and how smelly it was, but had never tried it. I asked the lady serving to open one and put the contents in a bag. I then cycled down the road for a while before stopping to eat it. The texture was thick, and it felt heavy. It was like biting into thick, stinky custard in a thin plastic bag. I didn't find the fruit smelly until I bit into it. I liked the taste, although not enough to ever want it again in my life.

I cycled just 28 miles to the Manee Sangkha Hotel in Surin so that I would arrive at the border for about lunchtime the following day. It rained most afternoons and through the night during my time in Thailand, so it was always great to get a place to stay before the heavens opened.

After an early night and plenty to eat, I cycled through farmland that was a little different. I saw haystacks, or what looked like haystacks, and there was a buffalo on a rope nearby, so I didn't get too close. The smaller roads on the way to the border appeared new and were super smooth. I stopped at a junction to check my map and noticed a troop of what looked like macaques dropping out of the trees like rotten fruit just yards away, and they didn't seem to care that I stood watching them, thankfully.

It felt amazing to reach the border. I spent an hour at immigration trying to explain why I didn't have a Thai departure card in my passport. I told them I didn't remember having a card, and if I had, I must have lost it. They then took photographs of me, and one of them made a phone call while staring at me.

It took some time but, once through, I set about looking for a hotel. Staff at the first hotel not far from the crossing told me to move the bike from outside the reception area, and that it wasn't allowed inside. At the second hotel a little farther on, I could only keep the bike behind the building. I felt I had no choice but to drop down from the plateau, and head deeper into Cambodia.

It was great to fly down the hill from the plateau, and the first thing I noticed was that the landscape wasn't as green as it was on the plateau and it seemed a lot poorer. There was a lot of litter everywhere. Little stalls I stopped at on the roadside didn't have refrigerators. They had big cool-boxes instead, filled with ice. They also sold what looked like plastic, fizzy drinks bottles full of home-brewed beer or spirits, but it turned out to be cheap petrol. I passed a lot of rickety houses built on stilts and thought they looked like the houses I'd seen in some old war movies. Cambodia was such a contrast from Thailand, and I hadn't even covered any real distance in Cambodia at that point. But I was greeted with lots of smiles and hellos in English, and I felt welcomed.

After battling fierce headwinds and covering about 22 miles, not counting the miles I had covered in Thailand that morning, I finally found some suitable digs. I didn't pass any of the lovely little resorts that were so numerous in Thailand. Those days seemed to have gone. In the Oddamratha Guesthouse in Samraong I had a basic room, but I was allowed to take the bike inside. After settling in, I went to the reception desk and asked if they sold beer, but they didn't. A staff member offered to get some for me though, and he brought back five cans of Cambodia's Angkor beer for roughly £2. I hadn't had a chance to get Cambodian currency, but thankfully the guesthouse took Thai Baht.

As I lay on my bed that night, I thought about how sometimes I took my achievement for granted. Just the thought that I was going to cycle 400 miles or so across Cambodia to Vietnam was an incredible feeling. There were many people back in the UK who thought I'd not make it to France or Spain, let alone cycle in India or Cambodia. There were times that I also had my doubts.

Given that I had such a long second day planned, I thought I'd better get off the guesthouse bed and see if I could find some shops to stock up on food and water. There were a lot of street food stalls and small, tatty restaurants along streets lined with rubbish, and none of them had food that looked nice to me. A lot of the time, I imagined the food to be fine, but conditions at times put me off. Often when I passed through the more deprived parts of a country, I thought about how fortunate my daughters were back in the UK, ticking along nicely. I felt sad when I saw girls the same age as mine at the roadside selling bits of next to nothing to survive, or toiling in the fields.

After about half an hour of wandering around town, I came across a small supermarket. An assistant said they didn't take Thai Baht, so I located a cash machine with options for cash in Cambodian Riel or US dollars. A security guard was standing next to the cash machine, and he told me to choose dollars. On returning to the supermarket, a different assistant said they didn't accept dollars, but did accept Thai Baht. I could have screamed. I bought biscuits and crisps and other junk for that evening, and some healthier items and water for the following day.

Knowing I had food and water for the day ahead was always a good feeling, as I never knew where I would end up or even how I would end up. The landscape looked okay for camping, but I had no intention of doing any. I was advised not to wild camp in Cambodia, Vietnam, and parts of Thailand close to some of the borders. The safest places to wild camp in Cambodia and Vietnam were said to be along the coast or on islands popular with tourists. Many millions of land mines and other unexploded weapons lay dormant, and many people were killed or maimed each year. I had lived more lives than nine cats, but I had no intention of taking such an unnecessary risk.

After 50 miles on my second day, I arrived in the town of Kralanh and located a guesthouse, but the bike had to stay outside. I had no idea what it was about the bike, but it was as though it meant nothing and was worthless. I still had about 35 miles to go to reach Siem Reap, but I was never going to make it that day. At the same time, I had little choice but to continue cycling in that direction in the hope of coming across another place to stay.

Just a few hundred yards farther on, and while still in Kralanh, I saw what looked like a small guesthouse. I couldn't read the wording, but 24/7 stood out like a sore thumb, so I crossed the road and asked. A shower and two cold beers down my neck later, bike in the room, and I was like a pig in shit. I didn't care that there weren't any windows. I didn't care about the dozens of mosquitoes on the walls. I was just happy to find a place to sleep, and I soon sorted the mosquitoes out with half a can of bug killer.

While the spray was going to work, I took a walk to a stall across the street selling fruit and vegetables which looked so tasty from a few yards away. As I got close, I could see hundreds of flies crawling all over everything, and it put me off. I managed to buy a SIM card in the town for buttons, and I was chuffed about that. Critters in the room dead, I was soon fast asleep and up early to make my way to Siem Reap.

The last time I'd taken a couple of rest days was back in Laos, so I looked forward to taking a few days off to visit Angkor Wat. After about 20 miles of cycling towards Siem Reap, my neck started playing up. It was as though I had a substantial weight on my head, pushing it down. Every few miles I had to stop to stand straight in an attempt to take the strain off my neck, and I took a fair few painkillers as well. I hadn't worn a helmet for a few days, only a headband to keep the sweat out of my eyes, so I knew it wasn't the weight of the helmet. I was glad I had planned a couple of days of rest; it was just what I needed.

On arrival in the city, it was just how I'd imagined; packed out with tourists and looking like loads of fun. I booked into the Mad Monkey Hostel online and messaged them to say I had a bike that needed to be kept secure, ideally in my room. On arrival, they told me I would have to leave the bike outside the grounds with the motorbikes and scooters, so I was pretty annoyed about that and told them so. I also waited while they cancelled my booking, and I made sure they didn't charge me. I then had a little ride around town and found a stunning hotel. It was more expensive than the hostel, but the price included breakfast. The Apsara Residence Hotel was worth every penny, and it was great to feel I didn't have to empty half a can of bug spray into the room. It also had a security guard and a spot in an underground car park for the bike.

After a great sleep, it was Angkor Wat day. The bike stayed in the underground car park while I hailed a tuk-tuk. The Angkor complex was massive, covering an area of about 400 acres, and there were so many temples. The big attraction was the Angkor Wat temple. My driver was great and he took no prisoners on the roads, bobbing and weaving in the traffic to make sure I got to see as much of the complex as possible. The only problem was that it rained heavily for much of the day, and although I was inside the carriage, he wasn't. To avoid getting rain in his face, he kept opening his umbrella and hiding behind it. He almost had my nerves gone. The entrance fee to the complex was about £28 and included all areas for a full day, which I thought was pretty high, but still worth it. I had a fantastic time.

After a great time in Siem Reap, I set out after breakfast from the lovely hotel, and even though I hadn't planned to cycle far, it was a hard day. I was on one long road; the National Highway 6 that ran from Siem Reap to Phnom Penh. It was dusty and dull, with coaches, buses, and all sorts of large vehicles getting far too close for comfort as they passed. Still, I made good time and arrived at some digs at 2.30 p.m. The first room offered was £3. It had a shower room, a single bed with some tatty sheets, and a TV, but no air-con; just a tiny ceiling fan, and a spider on the wall the size of my fist. I asked if they had a different room with air-con and no spider, and they did, for £6. The only problem was, it had the biggest gecko I had ever seen and it didn't seem to care that I was in the room in broad daylight, and I could have sworn it winked at me. I could only imagine how loud that thing would be in the night, but I felt better sleeping in a room with the gecko than the spider.

I did a little exploring near the guesthouse, but not for long. It was dusty and smelly, with rubbish everywhere and nothing worth seeing. I went back and had the guesthouse staff prepare a cup of instant noodles for me. I still had plenty of food in my bags that I'd bought in Siem Reap, so I wasn't going to starve. I awoke to find the gecko in the same spot. It appeared to have been there all night long, so I approached it and gave it a prod with a plastic fork. It sprung to life and startled me as it legged it.

I still had 160 miles to cycle to Phnom Penh, so I made an early start, and as soon as I left the town, women lined the roads selling hot sticky rice in bamboo. The women seemed dressed up with lots of make-up and big smiles. A little farther on, there appeared to be a whole town selling dried fish of all shapes and sizes. I had expected the road to be dusty and boring the entire way to Phnom Penh, but it was so exciting. Motorbikes went past with cages on the back containing all sorts of creatures, including colourful birds, piglets, and even animals that we in the UK thought of as pets. At one point, I saw something drop from the back of a motorbike. It turned out to be a small eel, wriggling on the hot tarmac, so I quickly pushed it into a rice paddy.

A few days later, I cycled into Phnom Penh where there was a big election scheduled. People were waving flags, bands were playing, and government officials in large motorcades went by. I pulled into a car wash and had the staff jet-wash all the thick dust and dirt off the bike. They then dried it off with towels, and it looked almost new. I couldn't turn up to a hotel with the bike covered in dust and expect it to be allowed inside.

The hotel I found, Le Safran de Phnom Penh, was lovely and in the heart of the city. The manager let me keep the bike in the grounds, under the watchful eyes of the security guards. Phnom Penh seemed just like a lot of big cities I'd visited. Poverty, wealth, hectic traffic. At night, the whole place lit up like a Christmas tree with lots of bars and restaurants. I ended up at a sports bar the first night, talking to a load of expats from around the world. It was a giggle for a few hours, and I had a great roast dinner with Yorkshire pudding and roast beef.

The next morning at my hotel in Phnom Penh, I jumped into a tuk-tuk and headed to Choeung Ek Genocidal Center.

Walking around The Killing Fields site felt very strange. Seeing the pits where thousands of people were killed and buried was so sad. But the most disturbing part for me was standing next to a tree known as The Killing Tree that soldiers swung children against to kill them. Visitors to the tree dropped wristbands and beads over a little fence that surrounded the tree to show their respect, then staff picked up the bands and added them to the others on the tree. I then asked the tuk-tuk driver to take me to Prison 21, or S-21 as it was also known, which was once a school before being turned into a torture and murder centre by the Khmer Rouge. I was provided with a headset to wear while walking around the prison, and the stories I heard through the earphones were shocking.

After another night at the sports bar and some great food and company, I was up and on the road the following morning quite early, heading for Vietnam. Cycling through the chaotic Phnom Penh traffic was great fun. Just a mile out of the city, women were selling giant snails at the roadside in baskets. I had never seen freshwater snails as big. Some were well over two inches across, and there were dozens of stalls, and mountains of snails. One woman said hello to me, so I stopped to look at the snails. I asked her if the snail-selling business was slow, and she just looked at me and smiled.

A few miles farther on, I stopped under a tree at the side of the road to check my phone and have a short rest. I could hear a kitten crying but

I couldn't see it anywhere, so I parked the bike and started looking in the long grass at the side of the road that also ran along the edge of a paddy field. I was at a loss, and just as I was about to cycle off, I focused on a large mound of empty snail shells under the tree in a ditch. Looking right at me with big blue eyes, was the tiniest of ginger kittens. I didn't know what to do. I thought it wouldn't stand a chance with all the snakes and critters in and around paddy fields, so I tried to reach it. As I got closer, the kitten got farther away, until it vanished in the grass. I could only hope it was okay.

About 30 miles into the day, I pulled up at a stall for some coconut milk and a bicycle tourist flew by. He looked over his shoulder after realising he had just passed me. How he didn't spot me from way back, I had no idea, given the size of me. He turned around and came back and introduced himself as Raymond from Taiwan. We had a good chat then cycled on together.

At one point I was in front of Raymond, and I looked behind but couldn't see him. I stopped and looked back down the road and could see him waving. He'd had his first puncture in thousands of miles. Not only that, but his rim had split around a spoke. As a result, the wheel was buckled slightly and was rubbing on the brake pads. I put my wheel building and truing course to good use again by helping Raymond correct the wheel. I had to be careful not to over-tighten the spokes and damage the rim further. We crossed the Neak Loeung Bridge, and I then spotted Lee Way Son Guesthouse. I told Raymond I was tired and couldn't possibly do a hundred miles more in a day. I wanted to book into the guesthouse. He was only in his early 20s and still had loads of energy, so he decided to carry on, but not before we had shared a couple of beers.

It was great having a little company for part of the day. I had just 65 miles to go to reach the Bavet Border Post, from where I hoped to buy a visa and cross into Vietnam.

CHAPTER 12

I could buy this, or do that

The dust was thick in the air as I cycled from Neak Loeung at a very early 6 a.m., and road conditions weren't the best to Krong Svay Rieng. There were speed bumps every few hundred yards in some places, making it hard to maintain a steady pace, and the shoulders of the road were mostly gravel and potholes.

But the day felt warm and pleasant. It seemed the farther from Thailand I got, the more tolerable the weather became. For much of my last day in Cambodia, I'd not only had warm weather, but I had the wind to my back and food in abundance. I couldn't have asked for a better day. But, by mid-afternoon and just 20 miles from the border, I completely ran out of steam. Luckily, I managed to find a guesthouse, where I had a quick shower and collapsed onto the bed without even bothering to fumigate. I was that exhausted.

I lay there thinking about how being able to go on a long-term adventure for months or years meant working hard, saving hard, and making financial sacrifices. Some people had to give up a lot to do the things they wanted to do. "I could buy this, or do that." "I could put my money into something, or do that." Those were the sorts of questions I'd imagined many people asked themselves before doing something incredible. They were the questions I'd asked myself. I had always felt that we didn't live once; we died once, and we had to make the most of every day we lived.

I hadn't finished what I wanted to do, so I prepared to head back to the UK to deal with a few financial matters, and to do a lot of juggling so that I could do what I set out to do. I planned to be in the UK for as short a time as possible, before returning to cycle Vietnam's Mekong Delta, along the Cambodian coastline and around the Gulf of Thailand, before crossing overland to Krabi and Ao Nang in southern Thailand. From there, I was just a few days away from Malaysia. My target, though, was Ao Nang, and once I set my sights on something, I was going for it: "shit or bust, all or nothing."

I hadn't seen my wife and children since before India, and I missed them after being away from them for so long. I decided to take Sue back to Vietnam with me for a little break. She worried a lot as I cycled through different countries, and felt I didn't care about my safety. She thought I was too trusting, not to mention a careless, fat-handed so-and-so who got up to mischief.

I understood before setting out on my adventure that I still had commitments and other things to maintain and manage. At 21 years old in the '80s, I gave up my job, my cat, apartment, relationship, and everything I owned before leaving the UK with less than £300 in my pocket. I didn't give a hoot about much back then, and I had no financial commitments or dependants. I took off and didn't return to the UK for two years, which were two of the most amazing years of my life. I visited Singapore for a few days and spent the rest of the time in Perth, Australia. I worked in brick factories stacking bricks, on building sites, and was even employed to teach breakdancing. I did anything I could to earn a crust so that I had money to splurge on having a great time, which I did.

Before I left the UK in the '80s, I was part of a robotic dance and break-dancing crew. We had regular bookings at nightclubs in Manchester, fashion shows and other events. So, with plenty of experience, I called into a dance studio in Perth and asked for a job. I had to do a little demonstration for the owners. They were so impressed that they took me on straight away. Before I knew it, I was flown out regularly to small towns in Western Australia to teach for days at a time. I was also in a television advert for an Australian company called Liquorland. I had to dress up as Santa Claus. In heavy black wellington boots, I had to perform a head-spin, a windmill, and my fluffy stick-on eyebrows kept falling off under the heat of the studio lights. As a young adult, it was easy to get up and go whenever or wherever I felt. Things were always going to be different once I had a wife and children. So, I was okay with my plan to return home briefly, and I was looking forward to it. I was also looking forward to getting back to Vietnam as quickly as I could.

The 20 miles in Cambodia to the border the next day was horrid. It was so busy, and the closer to Vietnam I got, the worse the traffic became. At times I was choking on dust and fumes, which left me chugging on my asthma inhaler for the first time in weeks. I got off the main road at one point, only to find myself on a muddy track and having to get back on the road I'd been trying to avoid.

While catching my breath, the second bicycle tourist I'd seen since Turkey came towards me as he headed in the opposite direction. He stopped for a chat, and I estimated he was in his late 30s. His bike looked much older. It appeared to be held together with string. He seemed the nicest of guys, but he looked like he'd been through hell. He'd been on his bicycle tour for a very long time and was on a super low budget. We talked about what we had been up to, and we had a bit of a laugh. Mark then set off towards Phnom Penh, while I continued to the Vietnamese border post. I would have loved to have followed his travels, but he didn't use social media or have a website. He was certainly doing his own thing, and I admired him for that.

At the border, I went to a counter and had a two-week visa stamped in my passport that would take me to the 10th of August, 2018. The guards then sent me through the building to an exit, but the bike was still out front, so I walked around the building to collect it and rode back around the building towards the crossing. There was suddenly a lot of shouting, and I saw lots of Chinese tourists to my right standing next to a bus, staring at me. I looked to the left and saw two guards with rifles rushing at me and shouting in Vietnamese. I slammed the brakes on and held a hand up while I reached into my bar-bag with the other. I held up my passport and pointed to the building. Another guy came over and must have told them what I meant with my gestures, and they waved me through. The Chinese tourists looked all happy and were a little too excited.

I felt I wouldn't make it to Ho Chi Minh City's District 1 before dark, because I was in such pain at both ends. My butt and my neck were giving me hell. I was in a bit of a mess. I came across the Blue Star Hotel, and I told the receptionist I needed a secure place for the bike. She said no problem, so I paid, but then found out the place she had in mind for the bike was the car park. I asked for my money back and walked the bike to the road, where a family wanted to chat and take a look at the bike. I asked them if there was another hotel nearby that could secure the bike. The daughter was sat on her scooter and said it wasn't far and she would show me. As I cycled behind her, her father was behind me on his motorcycle.

The Mai Vy Hotel had no problem taking the bike inside the building. They had a little indoor motorbike section with security, so I put the bike inside and locked it to a pipe. The father and daughter were kind, and I thanked them for their help and waved them off.

After getting changed in the hotel I nipped over to a mobile phone shop nearby, where the shop assistant refused to sell me a SIM card. He said it was because I didn't have a paper visa on my passport. I pointed to the visa stamp and said it was a visa and all I had. A second assistant shook his head and said "No way, José. No SIM card for you, my little child of a belly dancer's nightmare," or words to that effect in Vietnamese. I had no idea what he said, but there was plenty of head-shaking and attitude going on. The first assistant, who spoke English, said I needed a printed E-visa or some other form of printed visa. The situation had me wondering whether or not I had a valid visa stamped in my passport. I began to wonder if the guards at the crossing had confronted me because I hadn't completed the visa process. I was like that from time to time, overthinking things through having nobody to discuss problems or ideas with. I had to run everything by me, and I'd argue at times.

Despite stopping every few miles on my way to the city to rest my neck the next day, I made good time battling all the motorbikes and scooters that crowded the streets. The painkillers had stopped working effectively for the neck pain, and I was suffering. I booked into a hotel in the city in District 1 for one night, as I had my flight scheduled for the following morning at 6 a.m.

So, before going to the hotel, I dropped the bike and gear off at Saigon Storage. As Rohloff followed me on social media, they'd read that I needed storage for the bike and gear in Vietnam. They contacted a bike shop in the city and asked me to give the owner of the shop a call. Unfortunately, the owner was only able to look after the bike and not the gear. I needed somewhere to leave the panniers and contents too. I didn't want to lug it all to the UK and back again, because I planned on returning with some new tyres and more spares and clothing. It was still really kind of the shop owner and Rohloff to offer to help me out. I managed to locate Saigon

Storage, which was owned by an English expat, and he asked about my journey. He was impressed and offered to store everything free of charge.

Back when I rode for a little while with Raymond from Taiwan, he told me he would be in Ho Chi Minh City at the time I arrived there, so we'd agreed to meet up. He turned up at my hotel with a female friend he'd met in Thailand, and the three of us got chatting to a couple of girls from Sweden at the next table. It was great to end the day having a good laugh. I left the hotel the following morning and boarded a flight to Manchester, and what a great feeling it was not to be lugging the bike and gear.

As soon as I got home, I slapped on a load of testosterone gel and made an appointment to see the doctor over my neck. While that was getting sorted, I picked up spares for the bike and stocked up on thyroid meds and testosterone gel. I felt I couldn't continue to be without the gel for any longer, for fear of worsening the condition of my spine and joints. I thought I'd take my chances with airport customs.

The neck issue results came back, and it turned out I had arthritis in my neck. I was concerned the arthritis pain would make it hard for me to continue much farther than the Mekong Delta, but I was still going to give it my best shot to finish what I started.

Sue's brother, Ray, was working in Ho Chi Minh City at the time of our return. He worked all over the world but was in the city for long enough to spend some time with us. He invited us to stay in the spare room in an apartment he was sharing with his colleague, Jason. Sue hadn't seen Ray for a while, so it was an excellent opportunity for them to catch up.

On the flight with me was five months' supply of testosterone gel in pump-action plastic bottles - enough to fill one of my front pannier bags - and my new suitcase was big enough to put two 700x45 Marathon Plus tyres in without them twisting. I also crammed into the suitcase my very full Ortlieb Rack-Pack and loads of other bits. I'd used the rack-pack as a suitcase on my return to the UK. I was looking forward to trying out the Selle gel-filled saddle that I had tested on my old hybrid bike while back in the UK. It felt surprisingly good and was waterproof and sprung. Rain, damp or sweat getting into the leather Brooks bike saddle might have been the cause of the sores, for all I knew. Sue was concerned about my wounds because, one night while I was home, I left blood on the bed and a trail of blood from the bed to the toilet. It wasn't right, and I'd been sore for most of my journey. I kept hoping things would settle and I would adapt to the saddle, but I never did.

The testosterone gel sailed through customs in Vietnam. Sue and I planned to spend two weeks together, and I had no idea what would happen between the city and the Cambodian border, so I made sure to get a month-long visa. Leaving the airport, it was a beautiful sunny morning in Ho Chi Minh City, and we made our way to the Saigon Mansion Apartments in District 3. The two weeks we had together were great. We had a trip to the Cu Chi Tunnels, which were a massive network of tunnels built in a brutal war. We also flew out to Vietnam's Phu Quoc Island for five days. It was stunning in parts, and we lay on the beach every day. We then spent the rest of our time with my brother-in-law Ray, having great meals and drinks in popular restaurants and bars.

It was soon time to take Sue to the airport, and after a sad goodbye, I went back to Ray's to get my gear ready for setting off towards the Mekong Delta the following day.

A few days before Sue returned home, I took a cab to Saigon Storage to collect the bike so that I could change the tyres and get it ready. The tyre change was hard work. The Marathon Plus tyres were very rigid and much harder to put on the rims than the Supremes. I chose Marathon Plus because my route around the coast would mean riding over sharp shell shards and possibly a lot of broken glass, and I didn't think the Supremes would be up to it. There was a lot more weight in the Marathon Plus tyres, too. They didn't roll like the Supremes, and I had to put in a little more effort to turn the pedals. I wasn't too bothered about that because I wanted tough tyres for the coast, and if it meant few or no punctures, I felt it would be worth it.

Ray waved me off from his apartment early in the morning, on what was looking like a dry and sunny day. With it being so early in the morning, there were only about 40 motorcycles and scooters per square yard.

I was in no rush to overdo it on my first day back on the loaded bike, with new tyres and a very different saddle. I originally planned on doing just 20 miles, but I ended up doing 40, and I must have guzzled two gallons of water. It was so hot in the heavy traffic, fumes and dust, and the drain smells made me nauseous at times. Add to that a few dead things at the sides of the road, and it was tough going. It was great going over a few rivers in the Mekong Delta though, on ferries that charged just a few pence.

A lot of people wore simple dust masks over their noses and mouths, and back in Cambodia I felt it wasn't only because of traffic fumes. It was also because the dust in the air consisted of all sorts of nasties. People peed or worse at the sides of the road or in the bushes. They parked their motorbikes or cars and simply dropped their underwear, and they were good to go. That went for men, women and children of all ages. I was sometimes shocked to see grown women with their knickers around their ankles in broad daylight, and I was disgusted by men holding their plonkers for all to see. The dust had some pretty nasty things in it, for sure, and I put my bandana over my mouth and nose in some of the worst parts. I found the problem was worse in Vietnam than Cambodia, and not bad at all on the plateau in Thailand. I could only imagine what horrors I had inhaled.

On my way to digs that day, I had banh mi, which is a sort of small but fat Vietnamese baguette. It was much lighter in texture than the baguettes I was used to, and usually filled with things like meat, vegetables, chilli and all kinds of other things I wouldn't go near. I asked for two fried eggs on the bread and nothing else, but I turned my back for just a second, and the lady added some sauce and other lumpy stuff. I sighed and gave her the equivalent of about £1, which included a coffee. I took the banh mi a little farther down the road and lobbed it in a dustbin. I didn't have the heart to tell her I didn't want it. She looked so happy. I then bought another one from another seller, and I didn't take my eyes off her for a second. She didn't speak English, but it was easy enough to point to what I wanted. I tried to keep my street food simple, like deep-fried chicken, roti, and my new favourite: egg butties, Vietnamese style. Keeping things simple had saved me from falling ill.

At my hotel in My Tho, I had a well-earned shower and washed my clothes. There was no better feeling than sitting my butt cheeks down on a cold tile floor under a cold shower after a hard day in a hot saddle. That night, my host wanted to cook an evening meal for me, so I had pork soup and a bowl of rice and it was great. Sadly, there were about 15 other European guests who did all they could to ignore me after I'd nodded a friendly hello to them as they ate their evening meal. They could see I was on my own, but luckily I had got used to those sorts of shit-bags on my ride. After dinner, I went for a walk along a small tributary for a little explore.

The next morning, while getting ready to leave for Can Tho, the other guests saw me wheel the bike out of my room and suddenly took an interest. Likely cyclists themselves, I thought. I gave them an angry frown and went on my way. I tried not to let people like that get to me, but the more time I spent on my own, the more they got to me.

Earlier in the day, I'd stopped under the shade of a roadside tree for a few minutes for a drink and short rest. A friendly family approached me and insisted I sat down in their home across the road, where they prepared a fresh coconut and watermelon for me. It was such a lovely thing to do.

It was more than 60 miles to Can Tho, but I thought it would be worth putting in some extra effort to reach it in a day. I hoped to see the famous floating markets, so I needed to get to a hotel and book a tour for very early the following morning. It was hard going, but I made it just before the weather turned to thunderstorms and heavy rain. I found the TTC Hotel Premium Can Tho and, reluctantly at first, agreed the bike was to stay in the car park underneath the hotel. The staff insisted the guards on the entrance and exit would make sure it stayed put. It didn't stop me being a little concerned, because there was nothing to lock it to; it stood there in line with motorbikes, but the guards looked to be on the ball.

Later in the evening I went on the hunt for food, and there were lots of riverboats all lit up near the hotel, so I thought it would be nice to go on a small cruise for a couple of hours and have a meal. I boarded a boat, and a waiter plonked me at a table behind a large steel structure that was a part of the bow with no river view. I asked for a different table, but no joy; he told me the table I was at was the only one for me, so I left the boat and found a little restaurant down the road instead. I was up at 5 a.m. to get on the boat tour to the floating markets I'd booked for just £4, and it was worth every penny. It was a three-hour trip, and I was the only Western tourist out of about 30 people. They were so friendly, and we had a laugh.

I was back at the hotel in time for the most lavish breakfast I'd had in a long time, before diving into my fluffy white sheets. I'd booked two nights, because I wanted to see the floating markets and because the forecast was for heavy rain and storms. I was so glad I'd booked the extra night. I ended up staying in bed for most of the day. I had a bit of a fever for some reason and felt pretty sick. It was a shame, because I'd had such a wonderful morning at the markets.

In the evening, I thought I had better get some fresh air and try my luck with a different riverboat, so I crawled out of bed and made my way to the river. Once again, I was given another lousy seat, right next to a busy staircase. I still wasn't feeling well enough to be able to cope with people being in my face or banging into my table. I pointed to one that didn't have a great view but was in a better location. The waiter went into a strange panic and just stood there, seemingly shaking and unable to move in any direction. I looked at him and wondered if he was okay, or whether I was okay. All of a sudden, he ran down the other end of the boat and vanished. I thought he might have jumped over the side because I'd requested a better table. It was all a little strange, so I disembarked and went back to the restaurant I'd located the previous night.

The next morning I was still feeling poorly, but I didn't want to stay in the same hotel again; I needed to keep moving, even if it was for only a few miles. So I booked into the Mekong Rustic Can Tho, which was a sort of eco-lodge popular with young tourists, less than ten miles south. It was a pleasant, relaxing ride, and I stopped a few times along the river to rest due to feeling quite weak. After settling into a fabulous, self-contained unit at the lodge, I set about planning my route, because I still had about 120 miles to go to Ha Tien near the Vietnam-Cambodia border.

The landscape in the delta was different from anything I had experienced. It was pretty and deep green, and I loved all the small tributaries and lots of small humpback bridges I cycled over. There were so many different fruits and vegetables hanging from trees and bushes, and I often passed baskets of fresh produce at the roadsides with nobody around. It made me hungry to look at all the food, so I made regular stops to buy some fresh food at small stalls. I wouldn't have dreamt of stealing their products from the trees or unattended baskets. It was buttons to me, but not to the farmers.

Another thing that had my interest in the delta was the loud tweeting of lots of birds. It got intense at one point, so I stopped and looked in the direction of the noise. All I could see at first was a substantial concrete multi-storey building with small holes running around it. It turned out that the building was for swiftlet nest cultivation. The birds made the nest from saliva and, after poo and debris removal, the nests supposedly made for a great soup, which wasn't my idea of a great soup. The birds were free to come and go as they wanted, it seemed, and I started to see the buildings everywhere. Some hotels and houses had an extra floor on top with the birds going in and out. A local told me the swiftlets were non-migratory and ate a lot of mosquitoes and other bugs. He said the birds drank water out of the air, which was why they liked living in humid parts of the world. It was fascinating to watch them and hear a little bit about them, and it was a particularly enjoyable day. Unfortunately, the following day was not so good.

I wanted an early start for my last full day in Vietnam, so after a rough night in crummy digs, I set out in an attempt to cover nearly 70 miles to Ha Tien. It was roasting hot, and I couldn't seem to drink enough water. I also had a couple of coffees, a coke, and some fruit juice, and I swear I could hear myself sloshing as I pedalled. The road between Rach Gia and Ha Tien was one of the worst I had experienced. It was loud, dusty, and falling apart, but the worst thing about that stretch was air horns. Vehicles didn't just beep to say they were coming through, as they did in every other place I'd been; it was full-on, aggressive, and loud.

There was no need to use air horns to pass a cyclist, and certainly not on parts of the road where there was just me and the perpetrating vehicle. It honestly had my nerves gone. I still suffered from being hit by a truck, and I had been doing exceptionally well up to that point. I did my best to try to not think about what was coming up behind me, but the trucks seemed to wait until they were right behind me before unleashing. I kept jumping out of my skin. I knew it was a truck but I couldn't be sure the driver wasn't honking for a good reason, like trying to avoid something and wanting me out of the way quickly.

I didn't deal with it very well at all, and I would have loved to have unleashed on the drivers. I got to a point where I couldn't continue on that road, so I managed to find another route around the QL80 highway and got off as soon as I could. The backroad ran along a river and passed through some lovely spots. I stopped for an iced coffee at a small shop and got talking to the owner, who was a keen cyclist. He loved what I was doing, and he and his wife gave me a few bottles of water and offered to provide the coffee at no charge, but I insisted I paid.

Utterly drained, I still had a couple of hours to go to a catch a ferry that would take me across an estuary in Ha Tien. The QL80 had a bridge that would have saved me getting on a boat, but I didn't feel I wanted to get back on any part of that highway until I was ready to dash for the border. A couple of miles from the ferry terminal the road turned to a track, and as I bumped my way along, a small van passed, and the passenger threw a load of broken glass right in front of me. I had no time to avoid it and cycled right over it. I felt it crunching under the tyres, and my heart sank. I thought that, because there were so many big chunks of glass, the tyres would have shredded. To my surprise, the tyres did their job, and I had no punctures. I watched the van as it rode along the track, and I hoped it got a flat or broke down so that I could catch up and let the guy know how I was feeling.

I was soon at the ferry terminal, but it wasn't open. The bridge was my only real option, so I got on and off it as quickly as I could and located a great hotel that allowed the bike inside. The Bao Anh Motel felt like a five-star hotel and was only £12. I was so tired, but happy I'd made it to within four miles of the border. I stripped off, dived in the shower, and was asleep within minutes of my head hitting a fluffy white pillow. I awoke a few hours later and went out for a nice meal and a few well-deserved beers, and on my return to the hotel, I looked at my route through Cambodia to Thailand. It looked like there were some challenging parts ahead, and a stretch of road running through the Cardamom Mountains was undergoing some major reconstruction.

Crossing into Cambodia was relatively straightforward. The guards and staff on both sides were pleasant, and a few of them spoke English so we, more them than me, had a giggle over my size. It was around 9.30 a.m. at the crossing and quiet, and a couple of older European bicycle tourists were going in the opposite direction so I thought I'd have a chat to them. I went over and said hello but they only managed a smile in return, so I went a bit further and asked where their end destination was. The husband appeared reluctantly to respond before telling me it was Vietnam. He then turned around and started talking to his wife, who hadn't looked at me properly, so I gave up wasting my time. A little farther on and another bicycle tourist passed me going the other way, and he couldn't even bring himself to look in my direction. I had encountered more bicycle tourists like that than pleasant ones since starting my journey. I was so glad I wasn't like them.

From the border, I cycled 25 miles to the city of Kampot on the Preaek Tuek Chhu River, and on entering the town, I was delighted to see a Café Amazon. I had loved those places when I was in Thailand. They had air-con and great iced coffee, but there was a jobsworth parking attendant at the one in Kampot who refused to let my bike anywhere near the coffee shop. There was nowhere else I felt I could safely leave it, so I looked at the coffee shop staff who were looking at me through the window. I pointed to the parking attendant and shrugged my shoulders and left. It was far too hot that day for me to be bothered, and I only had another mile to cycle to some digs I'd booked online. I'd had a rough day.

Waking up to my first full day of three full days that I'd planned to have off in Kampot, I found it was chucking it down. At The Magic Sponge guesthouse, I had an upstairs room with a balcony, and it was spotless. At £20 a night though, it wasn't cheap, but the room was for six people and I wasn't sharing. I was permitted to leave the bike in the hotel's courtyard, but as soon as nobody was looking, I carted it up the stairs and put it in my room. I had no plans to use it during my stay.

The rain cleared before lunch, so I hired a scooter from across the street from the guesthouse. It had been years since I'd been on a motorbike or scooter, so I had to be careful. Cycling in and out of traffic since leaving the UK was good scooter prep, and it was just a matter of keeping my speed down. It was so easy to open the throttle and go for it. Best of all, my little Honda Airblade 150 was only £4 a day to hire, and fuel seemed cheaper than bottled water.

I had been looking forward to checking out some local attractions, and Sothy's Pepper Farm was on a dusty, bumpy gravel road. It was great fun to ride on a scooter, but I wouldn't have enjoyed it much on the bicycle. At the farm, I enjoyed a one-to-one tour with a young lady who worked there. She told me that Kampot pepper was world-famous because it was grown organically and in soils and weather conditions like nowhere else. She sat on the floor and showed me how they sorted through the peppercorns by hand.

After an informative hour at Sothy's I took a ride out to see some salt farms, which I found pretty dull. I stood looking across some fields watching a farmer driving a weird contraption up and down. It was like a golf cart, but instead of wheels, it had two large rollers. I could hear dogs barking, and spotted two gnarly-looking critters staring at me from a shed. As they started to walk towards me across a nicely flattened salt field, the farmer on the cart went crazy. He stood up and shouted at me while waving his arms, gesturing at me to leave so the dogs would stop crawling over his freshly pressed salt field.

My next stop that day was the coastal resort of Kep, which I thought wasn't up to much either. I did have a lovely meal at the famous Kep Crab Market though, where I met a couple who were touring on a tandem. They were much more pleasant than the other miseries I'd met as I crossed the border, and our short chat made my afternoon. Back in Kampot, I strapped my GoPro to my chest and did a scooter tour of the town, followed by a couple of beers while talking to some English expats in a bar. It was an enjoyable day, and soon time to eat some food. There was a special offer on at The Magic Sponge that night, which was a free pint of draught beer for every US$1 spent on food. That was my kind of special offer. I was starving. After shovelling a load of pub grub down my neck, washed down with free beer, I had an early night.

After a great night, I wanted to stay in bed a little longer the next morning because the sheets and blankets were so snug, and the air-con kept the room cold enough that I didn't want to get out of bed. By 9 a.m. I was bored with sleeping in, so I got a quick wash and went downstairs for a lovely full English breakfast. I then set out to see Bokor Hill Station, which was a collection of colonial buildings built on the Cardamom Mountains by the French. It was a fantastically enjoyable ride up to the hill station on super smooth, well-maintained tarmac, and the views from roughly 3,500ft were spectacular.

There wasn't much near the hill station, so I was quickly bored and headed back down. After about nine miles, I was roughly halfway down when I came across a westerner riding a lightweight road bike on his way up. He looked exhausted, so I stopped to chat and to see if he was okay and if he had enough water. He said he was on his last few drops. I'd passed a shop on my way down the hill, so I went back up and got him a couple of bottles of water.

I loved riding around on the scooter. I got to see so much in a short space of time, although I would often look at the map on my phone and spot a turn that I needed and then go straight past in no time at all and have to turn around. It was hard to get used to being on two wheels and going so fast. It was soon time to hand the scooter back.

My rest days in Kampot went by quickly, and it was time to hit the road again. I estimated I had roughly 150 miles to go to Thailand's border, and from what I could make of the terrain on the map, I felt it would take me about four days. The first half of the ride looked okay, but the second half looked lumpy. I said goodbye to my lovely room at The Magic Sponge and the owner and staff, and after a few checks on the bike to make sure there was nothing loose, I headed out.

After a few miles in hectic traffic, the road became less busy but a lot dustier, and later in the day there was nothing but roadworks. Krong Khemara Phoumin was only six miles from Thailand, so I set the town as my target. I hoped to spend the night there so that I would be able to cross into Thailand early the next day with tons of energy.

But Krong Khemara Phoumin was over 150 miles from Kampot. The endless roadworks and choking dust that turned the sun into a dull haze on my first day out of Kampot had me thinking the ride to the Thai border might not be as lovely as I'd hoped.

CHAPTER 13

Not a sausage

I was so glad I'd changed to Marathon Plus tyres and the Selle saddle. The terrain was relatively flat for the day, but the lack of tarmac, for the most part, made it tough going. I was exhausted by the time I located a shabby little resort-style hotel, but I had plenty of food in my panniers, so I had a good feed and flaked out.

As I cycled the coastal and low-lying sections, I passed some lovely looking fishing villages. Unfortunately, as I got closer, there were piles of rubbish everywhere. Being close to road verges, I got to see not only big items of trash but also the small things, like cigarette packets, bottle tops and straws. I got to see nearly every bit of crap, and it was sad. Sadder still was the regular stench of dead critters; most likely rats, I thought. I couldn't get the odour out of my nose, and it was sickening.

Ninety miles from Kampot, I arrived in Botum Sakor. As I looked ahead into the distance, I could see nothing but hills, so I expected a couple of days of some hard going, and I wasn't wrong.

Heavy rains had undermined parts of the road, and I wasn't able to make it to Krong Khemara Phoumin in a day from Botum Sakor. I fell 30 miles short and couldn't locate any digs. I had no choice but to pitch my tent in a clearing but behind a mountain of gravel. There was no way I was going to camp in the bushes, due to possibly finding unexploded ordnance or a nest of nasty critters. As soon as my head hit the pillow, I was out like a light. There were said to be some large animals in the Cardamom Mountains, including elephants and gaur, also known as Indian bison. But I was more concerned about the mischievous macaques. Thankfully I didn't see or hear any that night, and I was careful when packing up the tent to make sure there was nothing nasty underneath it.

I eventually cycled into Krong Khemara Phoumin, no doubt looking bedraggled and down on my luck. I was only about seven miles from Thailand, so I booked into a hotel. I then set about washing lots of clothes before hanging them on the balcony and the air-con unit, and the ceiling fan on low speed. I then went around the corner to Fat Sam's Restaurant for a feed and more than a few beers. As I entered the restaurant, I spotted a huge comfortable chair next to a small table. It was perfect, so I plonked my butt down and ordered some food and a beer. A few minutes later, a guy walked into the restaurant, and he seemed even taller and bigger than me. He looked me in the eyes and sat in a chair on the opposite side of the restaurant. We looked at each other and nodded hello. Fat Sam, I thought. It had to be Fat Sam, and I was in his chair. He came over and asked if he could join me, with us both eating on our own, and I agreed. We had a chat, and the food was excellent. He seemed like a great guy.

The next morning I headed for the border, then into Thailand with no problems at all. Immigration stamped my passport for two weeks, which was long enough, because I planned to get a visa extension in Hua Hin, roughly 400 miles around the coast. Four hundred miles was a much bigger distance than I had cycled through England when I first started at the beginning of August 2017, and that had taken me two weeks. I was only managing between 20 and 30 miles a day back then.

Once back in Thailand, the road conditions improved, and there were no potholes, hardly any traffic, and two lanes each way. There wasn't as much rubbish at the roadside, either. Slightly under four miles after crossing the border, I stopped at a little café and shop, where I picked up two bottles of water and a coke. I then realised I only had US dollars and Vietnamese dong. Luckily, the owner said it wasn't a problem, and I could have the items for free. I thanked him but told him I couldn't accept, but he insisted, and it was much appreciated. I felt the shop owner in Thailand was rewarding me for my good deed of giving the cyclist near Kampot a couple of bottles of water.

Later in the day, I found a great little resort, right next to the beach, and I was the only guest. I swam in the sea and had a beautiful swimming pool to myself, where I lined up a few beers along the edge, put on some music, and chilled. It was pure bliss.

The south-eastern corner of Thailand was quite beautiful, and my plan for the next day was to follow the coastline to Trat. I was up and down all day on lumpy stretches of road. It was like being on a rollercoaster. I'd build up speed on the downhill, then pedal like the clappers to get as high up on the other side as I could, then repeat, all day long. But I hadn't had a single puncture since I fitted the Marathon Plus tyres, and my butt had finally started to heal with the new saddle. I understood that people of average build or lighter might have been comfortable on the Brooks B17. I was more than 300 pounds and had a reasonably upright position when riding. It wasn't the saddle for me, so I left it next to a dustbin back in Kampot.

Another thing I found worked for my butt was removing the padding from the padded shorts. I was aware that it seemed a crazy thing to do, but because the new saddle was padded and sprung, I didn't think I needed the padding in the shorts. Using stretchy shorts without padding meant I didn't get wedgies like I would have done in a pair of boxer shorts, and everything stayed much drier. I felt I had cracked it and was on the mend.

After arriving in Trat, I thought about going to the coast to see if I could get over to the tourist island of Koh Chang. But the weather hadn't been great out at sea, so the water was quite murky and choppy. I didn't mind missing a few tourist spots, because I was seeing and experiencing amazing things every single day, and often without other tourists.

After a night in Trat at the Baanrimnam Resort Hotel, and a great meal of some of the tastiest duck I'd had in ages in a restaurant nearby, I continued around the coast towards Rayong. It was an enjoyable 50-mile ride, and I was grinning for most of the day. The landscape was beautiful, and I seemed to be surrounded by thick green vegetation and well-maintained gardens. At one point, I took a break and sat on a bench close to the road, when a gaggle of cyclists rode by on standard touring bikes and mountain bikes followed by a support van, and they waved and yelled hello. It was an organised tour they were on, so they had no gear to carry. It looked like a great way to see a country if time was limited, or for those not wanting to be on their own.

A little later, I passed those same cyclists as they sat at a small restaurant having lunch, then they overtook me as we approached a village. We converged at a road junction, and the group seemed confused, looking in all directions. From looking on the map earlier in the day, I had a picture in my head of a small bridge I needed to cross, so I cycled on past the others. They were even more confused than I thought, because they tagged on behind me, feeling sure I knew where I was going. I was usually pretty good at finding my way around, but the mob in tow had scrambled my brain a bit more. We hit a dead end and had to return to the junction to take another route. I could hear the growls. We eventually crossed the bridge, but I was so tired. That lot didn't have the gear to lug around as I did, and they were all at least half my weight. With all the panniers looking full to bursting, the villagers must have thought I was the sandwich boy.

It was back in Kampot that I'd had my last rest days, so I felt it was time to have a couple more. My original plan was to get a ferry to Ko Samet from Ban Phe. However, the water was still choppy and didn't look so great, so I found a fishing tackle shop and replaced my cheap, broken reel with an expensive one. Not that I'd caught a single fish during the whole adventure, but I lived in hope. I had planned on spending my rest days in Ban Phe, but I wasn't impressed, so I kept cycling.

A little farther on, I met a nice guy from Switzerland who was taking a ride on his bike. He lived in the area and was taking a short trip to Sabai Sabai Village, which was just a little farther along the coast. We rode together to Sabai Sabai Village, but I didn't like the idea of spending time there either. When it came to rest days, I considered them very special. I wanted at least nice digs in an okay place.

I ended up doing another 13 miles to Saeng Chan Beach after cycling through Rayong city. I'd spotted a Café Amazon in Rayong and thought it was worth a little detour. When I eventually arrived at the beach, I thought it was all a bit tatty. I decided to book into a cheap resort for just that night and planned to head to Bang Saray the next day, which was about 12 miles south of Pattaya. I didn't fancy spending rest days in Pattaya. I thought it would have been far too busy for me.

I was up and out early the next morning. The weather forecast was good, so I thought I'd go through some hills and green landscape instead of following the coast. It was effectively cutting off a corner and going a more direct but lumpy route. And what a ride it was! The roads were pristine, and I met some lovely people. I was offered free coffee and water by a couple running a small coffee and smoothie stand, and we had a good chat about my adventure.

In Bang Saray, I booked into Baan Chang Residence. The room was cheap, but I had clean white sheets, and there were no gaps under the door or around the window, so I didn't even bother to bug spray. There were times when a room looked tidy and clean, but as soon as the lights went out, mosquitoes would come out of their dark hiding spots and drive me scatty all night, not to mention other little beasties. After unpacking, I went for a wander and had a great pizza and a few beers with some expats. In the morning, there was a tasty, continental-style breakfast plus loads of boiled eggs. The breakfast had set me up for the day, and I was good to cover some distance.

I had roughly 40 miles to go to reach Bang Saen, and it was hectic on the roads. I tried to follow the coastline past Pattaya, but I continually hit dead ends and had to keep cycling up hills to get back on main roads. It was tiring. I stopped for a rest at one point and got talking to a UK expat. He was only a few years older than me, and he couldn't believe what I'd accomplished. I couldn't believe it myself at times. Jomtien Beach and Pattaya Beach were lovely but very busy; too busy for me.

At Bang Saen, I spotted a concrete jetty and fishing boats, so I thought I'd take a break and do a little fishing with my new reel. I sat at the end of the jetty for about an hour, fruitlessly fishing as usual, and I started to feel quite sad. I was missing my wife and children and feeling a little lonely and homesick. I missed talking to people for more than just a few minutes. I regularly spoke with others for very short amounts of time, but then they were gone. I was continually saying goodbye. I had said it far too many times. I'd been fine for a while, but as I sat dangling my legs over the jetty looking out to sea and not catching a sausage, I felt teary. I loved doing what I was doing, but I had been on my adventure for such a long time, carrying around all my clothes and gear to different places daily. It had started to become tiring and too routine. I have never been one for routine. I thought my feelings might have been a little mixed because I was about to pass Bangkok. In doing so, I'd complete the incredible loop which I'd roughly plotted months before in India. I felt I had a cheek to be feeling sad, given how lucky I was to be doing what I was doing but, sadly, I was.

Just as I was about to try to give myself a push, on the road and not into the water, a beautiful sweet little Thai girl aged about eight came over. She stood there looking at me with big, beautiful dark eyes the size of saucers, and I smiled and nodded. She started asking me all sorts of questions in the clearest of English, and it was lovely. She was like a little angel sent to kick me up the arse. Her mum and dad stood behind her as she chatted with the gentle giant on the jetty, but they spoke very little English. I would answer the little angel's questions, and she would translate to her parents. They then said goodbye, and I watched as they walked off the jetty and out of sight.

I decided I had done what I wanted to do, and I was going home for Christmas and hanging up my cycling Crocs. I was so happy with my achievement and had every right to be. But I wasn't going home until I'd hit the target I had given myself, which was to reach Ao Nang in the south-west, 600 miles away. While still on the jetty, I plotted a route, which was basically to continue following the coastline before crossing from the Gulf of Thailand to the Andaman Sea. From experience, I was fully aware that anything could happen during such a long ride. At least with me.

I felt a boost of energy and I jumped up, packed my completely point-less fishing tackle and hit the road. I carried on along highways, through industrial areas and heavy traffic, smelly dust, and underneath many miles of an overhead carriageway. At one point, I thought I was going to drop dead of exhaustion, but like a ray of sunshine, a Café Amazon appeared. I pulled in and had a large iced coffee and a couple of bottles of water. There was a couple in the café that were all togged up in cycling clothes, and we got talking and went outside to show each other our bikes. They were riding Thorn Cycles Nomads with Rohloff Speedhubs, but they were just out for a ride, so had no panniers.

Back in the UK, when I first started looking for the right bike, I had looked at the Nomad. The one I had looked at only had 26" wheels and no stands. I had read a lot of good things about Thorn Cycles. With bigger wheels and at least one stand, the Nomad might have been my choice.

The couple asked if they could cycle along for a while, and I agreed, but it was awkward at the same time. I had gotten so used to looking out for myself on the roads, that it was hard to look out for my two new friends as well. I sometimes crossed busy intersections, then remembered I wasn't on my own. I had learned to bob and weave in the craziest of traffic. I felt I was putting their safety at risk, so I stopped and told them I'd continue on my own. I said I found it hard to look after my safety while considering theirs. I knew they understood because they looked ever so relieved.

As the day progressed, the roads got busier. I spotted a large hotel and thought it had to be worth seeing if I could get a room. I didn't have the energy to keep my chunky legs going around for much longer. The manager of the Yamato Hotel in Mueang Samut Prakan District, found a space for the bike inside the hotel near reception. My room was excellent, and I later went out for a nice meal and to check out the hundreds of small market-style stalls that appeared after dark. I slept so well that I didn't wake up until 9 a.m. The centre of Bangkok was just 16 miles to the north of the hotel. The distance to the coast in the south was even less.

Before leaving the hotel I had a fantastic breakfast, and the manageress filled my bottles with ice-cold water. I'd located some digs just 30 miles away, and with me having such a late start, I decided to aim for that. I hadn't been on the road long when I arrived at Pak Nam Fresh Market. It was terrific, and there were foods of all kinds and some fish and shellfish that I'd never seen before. Mashed crab! Not for me.

Right near the market, I boarded a tiny ferry to cross Chao Phraya River. Although it was only a small passenger boat with no ramps or steps to get on, there was room for the bike. As we were about to leave, a Canadian guy dived in; he'd just left his hotel and wanted to do a little local exploring. We chatted until we reached the opposite bank, then parted company.

About an hour of cycling later, I stopped at a coffee shop, and the owners were lovely and offered me the coffee for free and gave me bottles of cold water as I was leaving.

Away from the heavy traffic and built-up areas, I found myself in a landscape of canals, rivers, and fish farms. At one point a small tractor with a trailer crawled past me, so I grabbed hold of the back for a free ride. The driver looked back because there was no way he couldn't have felt an extra 500 pounds yanking him back. I waved, he smiled, and we covered about three miles together. I let go because my arm was aching and it was boring.

The Chan Le Resort, where I chose to stay the night, was quite modern, and my room was on stilts in a shallow bay. If not for the cockroaches continually trying to get under the door from the wooden balcony in broad daylight, it would have been an okay place to stay for a few days. I used the resort's bathroom towels to fill the gap under the door after using nearly half a can of bug spray.

As I stepped out onto the decked balcony in the morning, the sea was like glass and the sky was cloudless, and small fishing boats appeared to be dragging nets close to shore. It was a stunning setting. I took my time packing the gear before heading to Samut Songkhram, which was about 35 miles away. As I meandered between the fish farms, I stopped for a moment to turn my Bluetooth speaker on and to find some relaxing music on my Sony mp3 player. Something to my left in the water caught my eye, and as I focused on some branches a few yards away near the bank, I saw a monitor lizard that must have been six feet long or more. I tried to get my camera out, but it vanished below the water. It was a fantastic start to the day.

I'd had surprisingly few tummy bugs since starting my adventure, and certainly not one that had caused me any problems. But on my way to Samut Songkhram, the shit hit the fan. I had no idea what might have caused the dicky tummy. It was either the food at the hotel the night before, or some lousy ice in a couple of iced coffees I'd had that day. It might have been due to all the fumes and dust I'd inhaled over those last few days coming up towards Bangkok.

I still wasn't feeling well the next day, but I was determined to push on. With breakfast included at the hotel, I asked for just two eggs over-easy, and I put them on toast. I chose to avoid coffee or fruit juice, and I continued through the day without drinking any water. I kept to sports drinks and sodas. I believed water was the worst thing to have with a bad tummy. In the afternoon, I had two cheese and ham toasties from a 7-Eleven, and by the end of the day I felt a lot better.

Hua Hin has a vast and beautiful stretch of coastline and is home to a lot of expats from all over the world. There are malls, bars, and all kinds of things to do that would keep me active for a couple of days, so I chose to have two days off so I could book a flight back to the UK from Krabi and extend my visa. The visa had to cover me for not only the distance I still had to ride, but also for a planned five days in Krabi and Ao Nang. Once there, I'd have to box the bike, buy prezzies for everyone, tidy up my gear, and hire another scooter to check out the area and take some photographs.

Lemon House 51 was a small, comfortable hotel situated in a part of Hua Hin with plenty going on, but not too much. I made myself comfortable in my room and then headed to immigration at the Bluport Mall, which was impressive. It had lots of familiar eateries and other restaurants and shops. Unfortunately, immigration wasn't open that day, but I didn't mind wandering around the mall and having a nice meal. There was a DHL courier service point in the mall, so I decided to post some gear home to lighten my load. I thought it would be a great idea to cycle as light as I could for the roughly 400 remaining miles. It would also make packing more manageable when I was due to fly home. I'd done with the tent, mattresses and sleeping bag, so I used the sleeping bag as packing material to protect the more valuable items. The DHL box wasn't big, but I crammed plenty into it.

I hadn't told my wife about my return at that point. I wanted her to think I was heading down into Malaysia over Christmas and New Year, and I wanted to surprise her. I managed to extend my visa and book a flight back to the UK for the 18th of December. I had a good rest in Hua Hin, but Ao Nang was a long way away, and I had to keep moving. The weather forecast for the following couple of weeks was for storms and flooding. I usually took weather warnings like that with a pinch of salt. I shouldn't have.

CHAPTER 14

Got a little wet

I had 80 miles to cycle to Prachuap Khiri Khan, so I gave myself two days to get there. I spent the first night in a small but clean resort with some shops nearby, and I was quite happy to give the beer a miss and just have an early night. I wanted to try to get plenty of sleep because I planned to cycle through Khao Sam Roi Yot National Park the next day and wanted time to enjoy it. There were some fascinating animals to see, I was told, such as fish-eating cats, barking deer, and crab-eating macaques. It sounded like the area had been a nuclear test site at some point.

So much for getting plenty of sleep. I had the most annoying geckos in my room, and they didn't mind making a racket with the lights on or off. They drove me scatty, so I staggered out of bed before sunrise and started cycling at first light.

Despite being tired, I enjoyed the ride for the first half of the day. Tall hills surrounded me as I rode some super smooth tarmac, and although I didn't see any fish-eating cats or barking deer, I did see a lot of macaques. Whether they were crab eaters or not I had no idea, but there were about a dozen of them getting stuck into whole pineapples. I stopped to watch them for a few minutes, but they were getting a bit too close to me, so I moved on.

During the afternoon, it started to rain. Luckily I managed to get to Prachuap Khiri Khan and locate a nice hotel before the wind, heavy rain, and thunderstorms hit. I dropped all my gear off and went to Ma-Prow Restaurant, which was a rustic little place on the beachfront. I had read online that the restaurant looked well overdue a refurb, but the food was excellent. Well, I thought the food was okay, and the place needed a rebuild, not a refurb.

Still, it was pretty typical, and I enjoyed sitting down for a meal and looking out at the sea as the storm whipped it up. After about half an hour, it was time to put up my trusty umbrella and make my way back to the hotel. That umbrella was robust; and it should have been too, for £35. I had bought it in the UK, and it was money well spent. I'd lost it and found it again, so many times.

All through the night, a massive storm battered the coastline while I lay snug as a bug in my king-sized bed watching the lightning. I left the hotel in the morning after breakfast, and there was damage everywhere. Palm branches were all over the roads, along with driftwood and other rubbish, and there was also a lot of building damage. I had been warned about the storm but I chose to ignore the warning, so I only had myself to blame. I felt I should have stayed in Hua Hin and given the bad weather a few days to subside so that I could enjoy the coastline, but it was far too late for that. So I battled on against wind and rain and, 42 miles later, I arrived at Ban Krut and some digs. I'd had enough for the day, and it was only 2 p.m. Thankfully, there didn't seem to be much in the way of wind and rain the next morning, and I felt I'd get to enjoy some coastline after all. I had avoided getting on a major road that ran along the hillside much higher up. Phet Kasem Road, or Thailand Route 4, was Thailand's longest highway at roughly 800 miles, running from Bangkok to the border with Malaysia. I didn't want to spend all my time on a busy road; I wanted to be near the sea and pass through little villages.

But, by 10 a.m., all hell broke loose. Torrential rain and thunderstorms were some of the worst I'd seen. Hills were shrouded in low cloud and mist and, due to all the rain, low-lying areas started to flood.

I started hitting roadblocks and diversions due to submerged roads, and each new route seemed to lead to another detour or roadblock. Road workers were unable to keep up with the flooding, and they sent people in all directions. Coconut palms swayed in the wind, and it got far too dangerous to be out on the bike. It was a nightmare and a little scary. I wasn't concerned I might lose my life, but I did feel I might lose my bike and gear.

As I continued, I found myself up to my knees in muddy water, and at one point I stood leaning on the bike and looking ahead as far as I could see to where there should have been a road. A few guys in pickup trucks passed me, with water up to their doors, and they had their tailgates down to avoid the backs of the trucks holding water. I tried to get their attention, hoping they would stop and give me a lift. Nope, just smiles and waves, and some guys thought it was hysterical.

The highway was eight miles of mostly uphill, and I needed to get to it as quickly and as safely as I could. I struggled to navigate because, every time I looked at my phone to check the map, I couldn't use the screen because my fingers were wet through and crinkly. I tried putting up my umbrella and wiping the screen with some dry clothing from my panniers, but I couldn't seem to get my fingers dry enough. Not being able to read the map, I became lost a couple of times. My best plan was just to keep heading upwards so that at some point I'd reach the highway. Thailand wasn't happy that I had planned to leave, I thought.

After what seemed an eternity I made it to the highway and I felt so relieved. About a mile later, I came across a large service area with shops and a small market, all under one enormous roof.

The first thing I did was make my way to the public toilets to get changed into some dry clothes from my fantastic Ortlieb panniers. There I met two other bicycle tourists taking shelter; one was from China and the other from South Korea. They had met each other a few days earlier and decided to ride together. We exchanged social media info before they set out in the heavy rain. They both looked so cold, with the guy from China shivering uncontrollably. They'd been in the storm all morning like me but, unlike me, they'd had the good sense to keep to the highway.

They both wore stretchy cycling clothes, so they were holding very little water. I, on the other hand, couldn't fit into stretchy tops, so all my clothes were saturated and heavy, and my fresh, dry clothes would end up the same in no time at all. Still, for some reason, I wasn't cold like the two racing snakes from China and South Korea. But I was, no doubt, half as fast and twice their weight combined. They had asked me to join them, but I would have held them up or been left behind within minutes. The only reason I changed into dry clothing was to make myself feel better for a few minutes, which I did. After waving them off, I had myself a lovely, hot coffee and some tasty, steaming hot food. I then waited at the services for two hours, hoping the weather would change, but there was no way it was letting up so I kept going.

It was tough cycling, but the wind had changed and helped me along. The guys I met at the services were heading for Chumphon and planned to stay there the night, which was a day's ride away for me, and there was no way I would have made it before dark. I managed a couple of hours in the rain before I ran out of steam.

Luckily, I ran out of steam outside a hotel. It looked derelict from the outside. On the inside, it looked worse. Prostitutes, I presumed, sat on benches in the reception area, seemingly waiting for customers. I didn't care. I was out of the rain and felt I was going to get a good night's sleep.

An hour after booking in, there was a knock on my room door. All I had on was a very long shirt that hung to just below my private parts, a few inches off the floor. Not quite, but it was long enough to keep me from blushing. I opened the door, but not all the way, and two women pushed past me. One appeared to be the manager and the other the receptionist who booked me in. I told them to hang on, but it didn't seem to matter to the manager as she proceeded to look all around the room and at my washing hanging from the curtain rails, air-con unit, and ceiling fan. She then asked if I wanted company. I looked angry and straight at the receptionist, who then appeared to tell the manager in Thai that I wasn't happy. She tugged on the manager's arm to get her out of the room, and they left.

The bedding was quite bad, so I slept in my silk sleeping bag liner. It was only thin, but it was better than the bedding. I used it quite often because it kept me surprisingly warm and bugs don't like silk, supposedly. I was exhausted and slept right through.

I wriggled out of my silk cocoon early. However, unlike a silkworm, there was no transformation. I was still exhausted and looked just as destroyed as I did when I got in, and I had sore legs and an aching back. It looked like it was going to be a sunny day to cycle into Chumphon, where I'd booked a room for the night at the Chalicha Resort.

I decided I couldn't keep the fact I was going home a secret from my wife. She had been missing me and thought she wouldn't see me for Christmas. I didn't want her to continue believing that, so I told her and she was over the moon. She told me she'd said to the girls in her shop I wouldn't be seeing her for Christmas. The girls told her I would. They had a feeling I'd be home.

It rained for the next two days, but not as heavily as it had previously. Although there wasn't much to see on the highway, and it was quite dull, I had no intention of straying from it until the weather picked up. I covered 110 miles over those two days and booked into Rhienchai Place in Surat Thani.

My original plan as I cycled around the Gulf of Thailand was to reach Surat Thani, then board a boat to Ko Samui and its neighbour, Ko Pha Ngan. I'd seen a lot of photographs of the islands, and they looked stunning. Unfortunately, the sea was going to remain rough, and the forecast was for another big storm. There was no point in wasting my time going out there. I felt sorry for all the people that had spent a fortune on package holidays, only to experience the islands in such lousy weather. I was disappointed too, but I still held out hopes of seeing Phi Phi, Ko Po Da Nok with its chicken rock, as well as Hong, Lanta, and Kai. So many famous islands to see in the Andaman Sea, depending on the weather.

The next morning, just before setting out to start my overland ride towards Krabi, I got a message from DHL. They were refusing to send the box of gear to the UK that I had left them in Hua Hin until I could answer a few questions. They wanted to know where I had bought the contents, what were they used for, when I'd left the EU. The list went on. They even threatened to charge me a daily storage fee until they were satisfied with my response. I was annoyed. Messages went back and forth, and in the end, I told them to open the bloody box and look for themselves.

The day I decided to go home, it passed through my mind to cycle back to Bangkok, which was just a short ride away, and head back to the UK from there, but I was still on a mission to complete my plan for Thailand. I wanted to get all the way down to Krabi and Ao Nang. I needed to feel I had done enough and achieved what I wanted to do. Anything less would have driven me scatty on my return home.

I continued out of Surat Thani in a bit of mood, but as I cycled a gentle but long climb, I got my big smile back. It was dry, the sun was out, and the tarmac was lovely and smooth. All I could hear was a slight chain rattle and the tyre treads crackling. I didn't know what it was about the sound of the chain, but I much preferred it over hardly any noise from the carbon belt. I felt connected to the bike, and it was a more natural feeling to be cranking away and getting a little feedback.

After leaving Surat Thani, I tried to keep to the more minor roads. I felt they were a better option in the improved weather, and I wanted to soak up some of the landscape on my final couple of days of cycling.

I was doing well and covering some distance. But, 46 miles from Surat Thani, I spotted a shortcut on the map that could cut seven miles off my ride to Krabi. After a few hundred metres of concrete, the not-so-short cut turned to a dusty gravel track, and then to a part that looked recently washed away. It was hard going for a little while, but I was so glad I took it. I cycled through rubber plantations and palm trees. It was stunning and quiet.

Thailand is said to be one of the world's leading rubber producers, and I passed a lot of plantations throughout the country. Pineapples growing under coconut trees were also another surprise to me; I had never seen pineapples still on the plants. The track turned back to concrete, and close to the end, I managed to buy some food from a small shop. I was just a few miles away from the last long road of my adventure, and less than 55 miles from Krabi. It was a great feeling, but I was also a little sad. As I sat eating yoghurt and some pineapple at the shop, I looked back over everywhere I'd been and everything I'd experienced. I struggled to put it all together. It felt too incredible.

After a rest and something to eat, I started down the 4037, and I was moving along nicely until I spotted storm clouds building in the distance heading my way. I thought I'd better find somewhere to stay before I ended up drenched, so I called into a shop and tried to describe needing a place to sleep. The shopkeeper understood and made a phone call. I had no idea what she was saying, or even if it had anything to do with me. When she came off the phone, she pointed down the road while nodding. I thought that maybe I wasn't far from a hotel, so I thanked her and went on my way, just as it started to rain.

I hadn't cycled more than a few hundred yards when I spotted a woman standing next to the road waving to me. When I caught up, she told me to follow her along a driveway. To my delight, there was a small and very basic resort. The lady at the shop had phoned ahead to the owner, who happened to be her sister, and she spoke excellent English. My room was about £7, and as the owner and another lady holding clean bedding and towels walked me over, they asked if I wanted one or both of them. I got a bit of shock and laughed and told them I was married. They started laughing and asked me if I wanted a beer. I said, "Now you're talking. Three bottles, please."

Just as I made myself comfortable, there was a massive clap of thunder, and within minutes the main car park area and driveway were flooded. I was so happy to be snug in my room.

I was out the door at 7 a.m. as the owner was hanging out some washing. She spotted me and looked startled and ran inside. She then came back out looking the same as she did when she went in, other than for a full set of gnashers that she appeared to be struggling to keep in her mouth. Bless her, I thought. She wished me well and waved me out of the drive. It was still raining, but only lightly, and I only had about 45 miles left to go.

Despite the light rain, I enjoyed the morning's ride, but I was starving. I hadn't had anything to eat since the late afternoon the day before. But, as

I entered Khao Phanom, my eyes lit up. There was a 7-Eleven and, within no time at all, I was sat on a step with two cheese and ham toasties, a bottle of milk, and a large hot coffee. I was then ready for anything.

The road conditions were excellent, and I received waves and smiles from people working the land and water. Not everyone smiled. One gent in his pond looked like he was ready to kill me. But I was sure he was only surprised to see me taking a snap.

A couple of miles short of my hotel, The River View in Krabi Town, I spotted a bikepacking bicycle in a window next to what appeared to be wedding dresses. I looked at the map and saw it was a bike shop: Mars Touring. Sadly, they had no boxes, so the owner of the shop got on the phone and located a shop some distance away that had one. I arranged to pick it up by taxi once I'd dropped everything off at the hotel.

The hotel was close to bars, restaurants, and markets. The manager didn't like the idea of the bike going up to my room on the second floor. She suggested I kept it near reception until I could take it apart and box it. She was concerned about oil or rubber marking the tiled floors, and I appreciated that. It was a lovely hotel. I'd never seen oil leaking from the bike, because the gearing was in the hub and swimming in oil that couldn't get out, and I used a dry lube on the chain that went on wet and sort of set like a soft wax. The chainglider kept all the grit and sand from getting on the chain and sticking to the lube, so everything always seemed clean. I only had to lube the chain once every thousand miles or so, if that.

I lobbed the panniers and gear in my hotel room and left the bike near the reception desk. I then went to a bike shop I had passed just around the corner from the hotel. It turned out they had a bike box two inches shorter in length than I needed, and they parted with it for just a few pounds. It was double-walled, thick cardboard, and I felt I could make everything fit. I then called the other shop and told them I'd got it sorted.

Back at the hotel, I took the box up to my room and put it on the balcony. I then went back down and started taking the bike apart. The manager was okay with me taking the parts up and putting them in the box. I started with the wheels, then the saddle and seat post, and when nobody was looking, I took up what was left and continued stripping it in the room. I washed each bike part in the big shower room I had. It took me a while to clean up after myself, but it was worth it. I put all the elements out on the balcony to let them dry, and I went to reception and asked the staff if they knew where I could get some packing tape and bubble wrap. One girl took off with the equivalent of a fiver and came back with the goods. After a bit of a struggle and plenty of padding it was job done, and I was ready to get something to eat, as usual.

The next morning, in Krabi Town, I took a cab to the airport to talk to Qatar Airways about the bike and box, and it went well. They put a note on my booking on the computer and told me to arrive early on the day of my departure to ensure there was room for it. Back in the town, the girls from the hotel managed to get me a couple of really cheap cases from a market and I was good to go.

It was sad to think of the bike all boxed. We had developed a bit of a friendship, although not to the point of being on first-name terms. After all the time we were together, I never thought of anything affectionate I could call the bike, as so many other bicycle tourists did for theirs. Bollocks was the first name I thought of, while it was in the back of a hire car on its way across France, and I called it that for a while. Not an affectionate name, though. I soon dropped that name shortly after Genoa in Italy and simply left it as the bike with no name.

It was soon time to leave the fantastic River View in Krabi Town and say goodbye to the staff. I threw everything in a taxi for the few miles to the Phra Nang Inn Hotel, which was right near the beach in Ao Nang, where I planned to pat myself on the back and have a few beers. I could have cycled the few miles to Ao Nang, but I thought I might have struggled to get a bike box in Ao Nang. I had no idea what to expect.

Krabi Town had everything I needed to get things sorted. I had no plans to do any cycling in Ao Nang: I planned on getting a scooter, and as soon I put everything in my room, I crossed the road to a scooter rental shop. I hired a bright yellow little 150cc Yamaha, and it looked new. I even had a parking space on the grounds of the hotel, close to reception.

I went down to the beach and sat on a bench and thought about the people who had donated to my chosen charity, JUMP. I was surprised that I hadn't managed to raise more than £500 in total. I'd heard of people getting a grand for shaving their heads. Still, every penny went to a great cause and was much appreciated.

Early the next morning, I received a message from my eldest daughter, Chelsea. "Up for a quick phone call I need to tell you something xx." Well, any parent would go straight into a panic, as I did. Whenever I had messages anything like that, it was rarely good news. Before I had the chance to phone, photographs came through, and my heart sank. Her fiancé, Bill, was driving, and she was in the passenger seat when their car had spun out in the fast lane on the motorway before flipping several times. The roof had flattened over both of them. Chelsea was severely bruised and had numerous cuts, and Bill had to spend time in hospital. I was devastated I wasn't in the UK when it happened, but thrilled they both got off so lightly. I was glad I'd be home in a few days.

I was quite sad that day, so I decided I'd go for a haircut. I needed a little TLC, but it was a big mistake. I was charged £7 for the worst haircut of my life. I rode back to the hotel at full throttle with my helmet hiding the damage. I did my best to correct it using my battery-powered shears so that I could at least pass as a $10 extra from The Walking Dead.

For the rest of my time in Ao Nang, I visited some beautiful islands and took some long rides out of town in the excellent weather.

While I sat at the airport waiting for my flight, I thought about my age and circumstances and health. I wondered how different the adventure would have been if I'd been in my 20s or 30s. If I'd been half the age I was, I'd have been much fitter and more likely to have slept on park benches rather than pay for digs. I was a lot different from that guy I once was, but I still loved a great adventure.

Stephen Peel

A highly unlikely bicycle tourist

Bicycle Touring Journal

Record everything

www.stephenpeel.co.uk